The Retiree's Social Security Guide

YOUR BLUEPRINT
TO MAXIMIZE MAILBOX INCOME

Joseph S. Lucey, CFP®

Secured Retirement Financial
MINNEAPOLIS, MINNESOTA
www.securedretirements.com

Joseph S. Lucey/Secured Retirement Financial
5775 Wayzata Blvd, Ste 830
St. Louis Park, MN 55416
www.securedretirements.com

Book layout ©2013 BookDesignTemplates.com

The Retiree's Social Security Guide/ Joseph S. Lucey. —2nd ed.
ISBN 9781795657891

Contents

Dedicated to my wife, Patty, and son, Gavin, who bring purpose and meaning to my daily work

Foreword
by Ed Slott

In retirement, income is everything.

Not just any income, but **guaranteed** income—not tied to the ebbs and flows of the stock market.

It's no longer about building savings, because savings can run out when you live a long life. Given today's increased life expectancy, it's essential that your money lasts as long as you do.

Social Security is a critical part of that equation and you need to be informed.

Financial advisor Joe Lucey has addressed this issue head on in **The Retiree's Social Security Guide**.

By guaranteed income, I mean your income cannot depend on your investments. Yes, the stock market returns over time, but sometimes you run out of time. Coming into retirement, you need more guarantees and less risk.

Social Security is what Joe Lucey calls "mailbox income," meaning dependable income. That's a secure feeling, knowing checks will be arriving in your mailbox every month, for life, no matter how old you get, how sick you get, or how the market performs.

Your Social Security benefits are mailbox income. But, even if you qualify for benefits, it's up to you to make sure you get the most you can. This requires planning and professional advice. That's exactly what you'll get here.

The amount you will receive depends on decisions you make about when to begin claiming your benefits. You want the plan that gives you the most for life.

The challenge is to be well-informed because the decisions you make are locked in for life. A mistake can cost you thousands every month for life. On the other hand, the right plan can **add** money to your monthly check.

The Retiree's Social Security Guide takes you through each step to help you make the decision that is best for your situation.

What you'll find inside is that the book moves easily through the basics of Social Security and all the options. Then it takes you through the planning phase of coordinating your benefits planning with tax planning to minimize your tax bill while maximizing your monthly income. The net effect is a bigger monthly check with less tax.

You won't get this kind of advice from most financial advisors and not at all from the people at the Social Security offices. They are nice enough and helpful too, but they are **not your advisors**. They only answer the questions you ask and don't offer specific advice for you. They won't point out strategies that you haven't thought of. They also won't warn you about the risks of a choice you may be contemplating. That's not their job.

As you go through the book, pay special attention to the valuable comparison examples. They highlight the stark differences that your claiming choices can make. Specifically look at the examples comparing the monthly benefits for twin brothers—"Bob and Larry." You'll see real numbers here that you can compare to your own. I found this eye-opening and easily relatable, and I think you will too.

In fact, you'll see how the advice in this book may increase your monthly check by hundreds of dollars every month, for life. That does not include the extra benefit of the income tax savings that can come from optimizing your IRA distributions by coordinating them with timing of your Social Security benefits.

The book also covers the two biggest retirement risks, besides taxes. These risks are living too long and losing a spouse.

There's a section in the book addressing death and divorce. That affects nearly everyone and requires special planning, too.

There's another section devoted to veterans. You'll learn how military pensions coordinate with Social Security benefits. You don't usually see this covered in Social Security books, but it's in this one. If this doesn't apply to you, please share this with a veteran who can benefit from this information, as a thank you!

Probably the best place to begin is at the end. First go to the **Glossary** at the end of the book where Joe identifies all the key terms you'll need to be familiar with. I think it will help you get more out of your read.

The bottom line is that Social Security decisions require professional advice. In this book, you'll be exposed to all the nuances, nooks and crannies and traps along the way.

As a member of ***Ed Slott's Master Elite IRA Advisor Group***, Joe Lucey has unique knowledge in the IRA tax planning area. This is a benefit to you in creating the largest monthly check going forward.

Maximizing your Social Security benefits is your right. This is not welfare. You earned this money and paid for it so you are entitled to get the most of what you are due.

Take advantage of the invaluable advice in this book.

It will keep paying off for you, every month, for the rest of your life!

Ed Slott, CPA, Retirement Expert
Founder of www.irahelp.com

CHAPTER 1

Helping the Fighter Pilot
See Through the Clouds

I didn't set out in life to become an "expert" on Social Security, much less to write a book on the subject.

I was selling securities for a major corporation in the financial services industry—in the years before I established my own Minneapolis-based company, Secured Retirement Financial, when I first began turning more of my attention to Social Security. I did so strictly as a way of assisting my father—a man with enough intelligence, skills, and courage as a Naval aviator to fly an F-4 Phantom fighter jet in the Vietnam War, but who, as he neared retirement, still needed some assistance in handling the myriad components of Social Security and retirement planning.

I found that somewhat amazing, and a bit disheartening.

Here was a proud man who graduated from the U.S. Naval Academy, a trained engineer who became a mid-level executive for a national defense firm; a truly smart guy who could figure most things out for himself and did most of his own investing based mainly on his own research. Yet, even with all this working for him, my dad soon found, as he neared retirement, he remained dumbfounded by many of the complex issues regarding Social Security.

Sure, he understood the basics, just as many people do.

He'd sat down with a representative from his local Social Security Administration (SSA) office and received some helpful basic information, but not the kind of real planning assistance he was seeking. I'm talking here about essential retirement planning issues such as dealing with the tax implications of Social Security, utilizing the advantages of spousal coordination, fully understanding survivor benefits. In short, he wanted to more fully comprehend the myriad ways of maximizing his Social Security benefits, something that can mean tens of thousands of dollars in total impact over the lifetime of a typical Social Security recipient.

He quickly knew it was time to seek professional help, something he rarely did as an investor. So, he turned to his son, a financial services professional who quickly found that he didn't have a lot of answers either.

I found that pretty disheartening as well.

You see, financial services companies don't spend much time, energy, or resources in training their people to do Social Security advising. Frankly, because such advice doesn't generate sales revenue, transaction-based financial companies don't see the need to invest the money necessary to bring their advisors fully up to snuff on the intricacies of what is the largest source of income in the retirement plans of many of their clients.

Beyond that, the Social Security Administration by law is not allowed to give advice. Its representatives in local, regional or national offices are not financial advisors. They will answer your specific questions about available options, but it's not their job to tell you if there is a more advantageous way to take the benefits you have coming to you.

I quickly saw I needed to start self-instructing and set out to learn everything I could about Social Security. Over the years of doing so, I also learned more about making the transformation from the accumulation phase of life—that time in our working years when we save and invest with an eye on a life when we no longer *have* to work—to the distribution phase we know in retirement.

The importance of "mailbox income"

Not that I didn't already appreciate the essential role Social Security plays in "mailbox income," which I define in part as income that doesn't have to earn money before it pays you. Unlike systematic withdrawals from retirement accounts invested in the stock market—accounts that must continually earn positive returns in order to pay you—"mailbox income" refers to the steady flow of payments that arrive each month in your mailbox (in another era) or, more likely, are deposited directly into your banking account today. You never have to worry about these dependable payments not being there.

Social Security is just one part—the biggest part for most people—of that steady retirement income. Payments from defined-benefit pensions—for those lucky to still have one of that diminishing breed—are another example. Annuity payments also belong in this group, as this is income guaranteed by the claims-paying ability of the insurance company that contractually promises to turn your annuity premiums into regular income payments for as long as your contract designates. Regular income from rental property and revenue-producing real estate, farm income, or other sources also figures in here.

Keep in mind that not all of the preceding sources of retirement income can be considered "guaranteed." We've seen in recent years how some private industry pension funds are considerably underfunded, and the sub-prime mortgage bubble burst of 2007-09 demonstrated the sometimes-volatile nature of real estate as an income producer.

It's a long-held staple of retirement planning that steady, reliable income streams are a key to a financially stable life after we leave the everyday workforce.

This "mailbox income" is supplemented by money we've saved and invested during our working years. Such savings and investments are another critical piece in retirement planning, as anyone planning to live on Social Security alone is likely to be greatly disappointed. Hopefully, the investment markets have done well for you over the years and you've experienced solid compounded growth. But, you can hardly build an entire retirement income plan on this money.

The problem with at-risk invested money, of course, is its exposure to the ebbs and flows of the stock market, bond market, or real estate markets in which it is invested. This problem becomes especially pronounced as we make the transition from the accumulation phase of life to the distribution phase, when we turn those investment assets into income we hope will last throughout our retirement years.

Now, it's fine to have some exposure to market risk in retirement—depending, of course, on your personal risk tolerance and willingness to accept possible losses. But you don't want to be totally dependent on any one pool of money that can fall in value at any time due to an unexpected international incident, natural disaster, political change, or mere uncertainty in the market.

Even without such events, market downturns are inevitable, and they in turn can lead to restless nights for retirees who worry about living longer than their pool of retirement money that is suddenly springing Titanic-caliber leaks. Decisions made in trying to rescue such market-based assets are often bad decisions when done during times of tension or panic.

Among the many things I've learned in more than two decades in the financial services industry, I've learned that retirees with consistent "mailbox income" are usually less inclined to make the kind of bad market-driven decisions described above. Because their monthly income needs are not tied to the performance of the stock market, they have no reason to make risky bets. Such people usually find it easier to avoid breaking one of my cardinal rules of investing: "Don't risk the money you need as essential income." Or, to put it another way, "Don't take your mortgage money to the casino."

What we hope to accomplish here

This brings us back to Social Security and the purpose of this book, my first attempt to help people better understand both the basic workings of Social Security as well as some of its more complex aspects.

Two points to be made at the outset.

Since its Depression-Era establishment as a national retirement program—designed in part to encourage older workers to retire so younger workers could fill their hard-to-find jobs—Social Security also evolved into a financial safety net for people with disabilities. An entire book can be written on the Supplemental Security Income (SSI) part of the program that provides benefits for people of all ages who have disabilities, but this book will deal exclusively with retirement benefits offered through the Old Age Survivors Disability Insurance (OASDI) part of the program.

Secondly, some of the options and strategies discussed in upcoming chapters may not be realistically available to everyone. Many options we will discuss are mainly for people who have work or retirement resources to carry them through to a point later in life when they can elect to begin receiving Social Security benefits in a more advantageous manner. Many of the strategies we will discuss may not be appropriate for people who have not saved or invested and do not have retirement income beyond Social Security. We'll talk in a later chapter about how people with few retirement resources can help themselves by working longer.

My hope here is to educate you to the point that you can make better decisions for yourself, or at least ask the right questions when you sit down with a professional such as myself who can help you make those decisions.

This book will not attempt to offer situation-specific advice. As every individual's situation is different, no "conventional wisdom" can apply to everyone. Again, the goal here is to provide education on both the basics of Social Security as well as some advanced options not typically covered by the helpful but elemental guides the SSA sends to people about to become eligible for Social Security.

That said, allow me to offer one piece of general advice here at the outset.

I can't emphasize enough the importance of seeking fully qualified professional help before making major decisions that can positively or negatively affect the total amount of prospective Social Security benefits—a number sometimes containing seven digits for couples with two high earners—you might receive over your lifetime.

Consider, for example, the all-important decision on when to begin taking Social Security benefits. This first decision you make establishes a benefit level that stays with you for the rest of your life. Needless to say, you'll want to fully understand all the long-term financial implications before making this choice. We'll talk in more detail in later chapters about the different levels of benefits paid out when benefits are first taken at early retirement age as opposed to taking them upon reaching full retirement age, or even in years after reaching full retirement age.

We'll also talk in this book's final chapter about how to find professional help, but let's once again note briefly here my concern that not all retirement planners are as well versed on the subject as they should be.

Don't misunderstand me. A broker may be very skilled in advising you on investments designed to help you reach your retirement goals, and that broker will likely have a basic knowledge of Social Security. You might love what your broker has done in growing your investment portfolio, and nothing I say here should take away from a relationship you have with an investment professional you trust.

Still, I also must acknowledge that many—dare I say, "most"—investment professionals are not as knowledgeable about maximizing Social Security benefits as they are in explaining the advantages of stocks, bonds, mutual funds, exchange-traded funds, annuities and other financial products. Over my twenty-plus years' experience, I've found that, as people enter this critical stage of life called retirement—a twenty- or thirty-year period of unemployment—families need more than investment selection advice. They should be looking at how their different investment products coordinate together in a larger financial planning picture that should also include lifetime income generation, tax-efficient strategies, health care planning, wealth transfer in estate planning, and risk avoidance.

Again, to really receive the counsel you want on maximizing the benefits you will receive for life, you sometimes need to seek a second opinion, just as you would in consulting a medical specialist.

I'll talk in deeply personal terms later about how I developed a lifelong appreciation for medical specialists following the premature birth of my son—a healthy pre-teen athlete today. But for now, let's close this discussion by simply saying sometimes you need a financial specialist, especially when dealing with the myriad options available in Social Security. Hopefully, this book will give you some insight on questions you might want to ask of an advisor to make sure he or she is a specialist who can address your concerns.

The changing landscape of Social Security

Keep in mind, too, nothing here is written in stone. The Social Security landscape is an ever changing one.

When the writing of this book began in 2017, for instance, retirement planners such as myself were just starting to deal with changes to two longstanding and very popular spousal coordination strategies—the ending of the "file and suspend" benefits option, and changes to applying for spousal benefits through the "restricted application" process. These changes, part of a 2015 law passed by a Republican Congress and signed by a Democrat president, left advisors scrambling for new advice to future Social Security recipients who had hoped to utilize these benefits-maximizing options but were now ineligible to do so. (With some exceptions; more on this in an upcoming chapter.)

As the 2019 edition of this book is being finished in winter 2018, America is currently dealing with another Congress seemingly more intent than ever on making major changes to Social Security. Whether significant changes can ever pass Congressional muster or be signed into law by newly elected President Donald Trump—who, as a candidate, said he opposed major changes to Social Security—remains to be seen as of this writing. But allow me one personal prediction here.

Despite reasonable concerns about the long-term financial solvency of Social Security, I still believe this to be a program that will be with us for a long time. Social Security has become such a staple of retirement planning—a trust fund into which American workers have been paying for years, and from which they will demand a return—that I view it as almost "too big to fail."

There may ultimately be significant changes, to be sure. Future recipients may have to work longer before reaching full retirement age. The Federal Insurance Contributions Act (FICA) withdrawals may someday take bigger chunks from your paycheck. Cost-of-living adjustments may change or even disappear. Beyond that, the dangerous implications of privatizing Social Security— that is, taking at least parts of it out of the government's hands— rears its head with each change of political power in Washington.

Still, while I can't predict the future of Social Security any more than I can forecast the rise and fall of the stock market, I do believe America's government-backed retirement program will be around for future generations. That's why I'm taking the time to write a book about the Social Security system as we know it today.

We'll start with the basics of Social Security: How you become eligible to receive it, how you earn work credits, how you can learn what your projected benefit will be.

We'll examine how rules in place today affect the all-important decision about when to first begin taking Social Security. We'll explain the reduced benefit paid to those who begin taking Social Security at the earliest possible age (sixty-two, or even earlier at age sixty if you are a widow, widower or disabled); the full benefit paid at full retirement age (once sixty-five, now sixty-six and soon to be sixty-seven for most first-time recipients); and the enhanced benefit available to those who wait until as late as age seventy to begin taking benefits.

We'll look at how these first decisions can ultimately affect the total amount of Social Security benefits a recipient might receive over a lifetime—an amount dependent, of course, on the recipient's longevity.

We'll talk in future chapters about the tax consequences of Social Security, and the different levels at which it is taxed. We'll look at whether it is more tax advantageous to take income from Social Security or an IRA. We'll consider the implications of continuing to work while receiving Social Security.

We'll devote a chapter to the changing landscape of spousal coordination and options still available to some for this benefits-maximizing strategy. We'll also discuss survivor benefits and look at some common mistakes made in Social Security planning.

Making good decisions today about an uncertain future

I'm not going to kid myself and suggest this book will answer all your Social Security questions.

That's because so much of Social Security involves uncertainty. How much you ultimately receive from the program depends on:

1) How long you worked, which may be water under the bridge for many reading this book.
2) How long you live, which is something over which we have little to absolutely no control.

Really, the only aspect of Social Security over which you have any control is the decision on when to begin taking benefits. Dealing with that decision will be a major component of this book.

What we hope to do here is provide education that helps you make the most informed decision you can about an admittedly uncertain future. You want to be able to make decisions for the right reasons, even though you know the outcome might not turn out exactly the way you planned.

What do I mean by that? I mean you can lay out the best plan in the world, one with the potential to maximize your total benefit after you start taking benefits later in life rather than earlier, or take spousal benefits at an opportune time. But then you leave us just a short time later, which means you also leave a pile of unclaimed money on the table.

Or, you may have good reason to believe you won't live a long time because of health concerns or family history. You start taking a reduced benefit early, figuring a smaller piece of the pie is better than no pie at all. Then you surprise yourself by living longer than you ever imagined. Congrats on your longevity, but you missed out on a significant pile of money you could have had coming to you.

It's a little like planning a road trip. You can study all possible travel routes and pick one involving the least amount of time only to find unforeseen accidents or road construction that brings your trip to a standstill. Not much you can do about things out of your control, even though you made good decisions based on the best information available before you hit the road.

But making good decisions is all you can hope to do, and I hope to help in that process. Your road in retirement might not end up exactly where you planned because of things you can't control, but you should at least feel good about the decisions you made when preparing to start down the road.

I hope that by the end of this book you are more informed about the way Social Security works and, in doing so, have a better idea of the questions to ask when seeking help on options and strategies that can help make the most of the benefits you have rightfully earned.

If nothing else, I hope you'll realize after reading this that, if the complexities of Social Security become too overwhelming, there are specialists such as myself and my team available to help navigate this twisting road. Social Security, after all, is the largest income-producing asset available to many people in retirement—the only asset, sadly, for many. Why not work to make it the most productive asset it can be?

CHAPTER 2

Maximizing Benefits: Get the Biggest Bang from Your Bucks

S uppose I was to tell you that, as a typical American worker nearing or considering retirement, there was a pool of potential money conservatively estimated to be somewhere around $352,800 waiting for you on what reasonably can be called your life's horizon? Got your attention yet?

No, this isn't a trick question.

The above figure is derived by taking the average monthly Social Security benefit paid to all retired workers—which in January 2019 is projected to be $1,470, as determined by the Social Security Administration—and multiplying it by twelve months to get a $17,640 average annual total.[1] We then multiply that amount by 20 years, the time period for which the average Social Security recipient can expect to receive benefits, according to SSA reports.

A number like this sometimes comes as a shock to people who don't look at much beyond the monthly benefit they will receive. They are, quite simply, failing to see the big picture of what Social Security means in planning for retirement income.

---

[1] Social Security Administration. 2018.. "2019 Social Security Changes." https://www.ssa.gov/news/press/factsheets/colafacts2019.pdf.

Let's add even more perspective to this big picture.

The conservative estimate cited above represents a twenty-year projection—one that does not include possible cost-of-living adjustments (COLAs)—that might be paid to a single earner receiving the average monthly benefit at full retirement age (FRA). For a married couple, that $336,960 estimate might well be compounded to 1.5 to two times its initial value.

Let's go even further here and note that many readers of this book—and I would say most—will receive a monthly benefit considerably larger than the SSA's calculation of $1,470 as the average for all Social Security recipients. In fact, most of the folks we see in our Minneapolis office tend to be higher earners whose monthly Social Security benefit at FRA typically exceeds $2,000. Why is this? Well, those who tend to be a little more educated often earn more over their lifetimes, as well as paying more attention to their retirement planning—often by reading material such as this book. They consequently are in a better position to make strategic planning decisions that can have significant impact on their total retirement income.

To put some monetary perspective on this, a person receiving a $2,000 monthly benefit at FRA might see—if he or she lives long enough—total Social Security payments of $480,000 (before COLAs) after twenty years. That total might grow even larger for persons deferring benefits for several years after reaching FRA.

Frankly, it's not unusual in our office to see couples looking at a prospective seven-digit total benefits pool. This is especially true for a couple who was proactive in preparing for retirement. Such people can typically rely on income other than Social Security that allows them to pursue maximizing strategies not often available to people who have little retirement income beyond Social Security.

Taking benefits at age sixty-two, sixty-six, sixty-seven, or seventy

For the purpose of illustration in this chapter, however, let's look at a prospective retiree who will wait until age sixty-six—full retirement age for baby boomers born between 1943 and 1954—before he starts taking what the SSA says is the average $1,470 full monthly benefit that might ultimately produce the twenty-year total payout of $352,800 cited earlier.

(I say "might," because the payout will be less if you live fewer than twenty years in retirement. But, that payout also could be larger if you take Social Security for more than twenty years. Here's wishing you the latter of those two prospects!)

Now let's put that same baby boomer into another typical scenario.

The boomer described above now exercises the option to begin taking Social Security benefits four years earlier, at age sixty-two. He or she is perfectly entitled to do so, but this decision comes with a price they will pay for the rest of their life.

Their projected monthly benefit of $1,470 at FRA will be reduced by up to 25 percent—for a person taking the full forty-eight months of "early" payments—to a figure of around $1,102.5 a month.[2] Their annual benefit is now $13,230, down from the $17,640 annual payment they would have received had they waited until FRA. Their projected total payout after twenty years is reduced to around $264,720. If they live to age eighty-six—the same age as the above recipient who has been getting payments for twenty years since starting at age sixty-six—their total payment

---

[2] The 25 percent reduction in benefit for "early retirement" is based on a full 48 months of benefits taken before FRA. As a person reduces the length of time during which he takes early benefits, so too does he reduce the percentage of reduction. The reduction rate is 5/9 of 1 percent for the first 36 months, and 5/12 of 1 percent for each additional month.

over twenty-four years rises to $317,520, still some $35,300 short of the FRA total, even though they received four more years of payments.[3] [4]

Let's look at one more scenario, this one with a more upbeat tone.

You are now the same baby boomer as above, but now you have the retirement resources and patience to wait until age seventy before you start taking benefits. Congrats, you have a bonus coming your way. For, through the process of "delayed retirement credits," your benefit is growing at a rate of 8 percent each year from the time of FRA until you begin taking benefits, or age seventy, whichever comes first.

If our above person with an FRA of sixty-six delays benefits until age seventy—the latest he can accumulate deferred credits—his monthly benefit rises 32 percent from $1,470 to $1,940 and his annual total from $17,640 at age sixty-six to $23,280 at age seventy. At age eighty-six, after taking only sixteen years of benefits, his total payout is $372,480—$54,960 more at the same age than his friend who took benefits beginning at FRA. If our late starter is fortunate enough to receive payments for twenty years, his total payout at age ninety will be over $465,600.[5]

Make the most of what you are due

The figures above are used for illustration purposes only. Everyone's monthly benefit varies depending on career earnings in

---

[3] Social Security Administration. 2018. "Benefit Reduction for Early Retirement." https://www.ssa.gov/oact/quickcalc/earlyretire.html.

[4] The reduction rate increases for people born in 1960 or later, which likely will include many readers here. With their FRA moving to age 67, their period of taking a reduced benefit if starting at age 62 increases to five years from four, and to 60 months from 48. The reduction from their full benefit could be as high as 30 percent.

[5] None of the above estimates include cost-of-living adjustments.

their Primary Insurance Amount, which serves as the basis in determining a monthly Social Security benefit. Many people will fare better than our above example; others not as well. Remember, these figures are based on what the SSA says was the average monthly benefit paid in early 2019.

So, everyone's benefit payment will vary. Yet, everyone with money in the Social Security pool has this in common.

You've got money coming to you at some point later in life. This is money Uncle Sam owes you, money he's been taking from your paycheck since a time when acne was your main concern. He's taken it legally with the promise that he'll pay you back at a time later in your life when you no longer choose to work.

This money is not welfare or a government subsidy. You've paid for years into a social insurance program, and you are due a return on that investment. Take no offense if you hear politicians call this an "entitlement program." It's an entitlement only in that you are "entitled" to something that is yours.

Let's add even more perspective on this "entitlement."

Keep in mind that you've been making a contribution of 6.2 percent of every paycheck to Social Security. Moreover, your employer is making a matching contribution of that same 6.2 percent for a total payroll contribution of 12.4 percent each paycheck. That contribution far exceeds the average American's contribution into a retirement plan such as an IRA, 401(k) or 403(b). It is entirely likely, in fact, that you have paid more into the Social Security "annuity" than you have into all your other retirement accounts combined. You are more than "entitled," you in fact deserve to wring every nickel you can from this benefit.

Now consider this. As long as you have this money coming and you have options available in the ways you receive it, why not plan to take it in the most advantageous way?

As the largest piece of the retirement puzzle for most people— and the only piece, sadly, for far too many—Social Security income deserves the same kind of attention you give to stocks, bonds, CDs, insurance, inheritance, real estate, or any other asset upon which you are counting for future income after regular payroll checks stop arriving.

Yet, for too many people, Social Security planning is reduced to a question of "When do I sign up and how much will my benefit be?" I've seen far too many people come through my office with carefully prepared spreadsheets showing "breakeven points," the juncture at which total Social Security benefit payments become equal whether taken early, at full retirement age, or at age seventy. They say they've detailed their monthly expenses, weighed them against a monthly benefit from early Social Security and determined, "I can live on this."

Well, I commend these folks for doing at least some planning. But I fear they're still not seeing the big picture, especially in how that first decision on when to begin taking benefits affects other Social Security options available further down the road. Or, they fail to fully appreciate the impact of Social Security on taxes in retirement—perhaps the second-biggest drain (behind health care) on a retirement nest egg. Or, as noted above at the start of this chapter, they don't see the impact a reduced or an enhanced benefit can have on your total retirement income.

Some of them end up doing the wrong thing for well-intentioned reasons.

Many well-meaning men I've met elect to start taking benefits early, hoping to do what is best for their family. Sadly, they often end up doing just the opposite. They believe by taking benefits as soon as possible, at age sixty-two, they will increase the family's cash flow and help the monthly budget. What they fail to consider is that, in most marriages, the husband is going to die before his wife—the U.S. Census Bureau says about 80 percent of women outlive their spouses.[6] Because he took a reduced benefit early, he inadvertently shot her in the foot by leaving her a lower survivor benefit at a time when she may struggle to replace his lost income. We'll talk more about survivor benefits in Chapter 8.

The magnitude of risk

To be sure, we make many decisions in financial planning, and not all of them turn out to be good ones. This doesn't make them a killer in the overall success of our retirement. It's not going to break you, for instance, if you sell a stock too early or lose almost everything on a $2,000 investment. You can recover over time from those kinds of decisions.

But, when you start messing up on things like Social Security benefits, these are big mistakes that can't be reversed.

I like to use the following example with clients.

I ask them to imagine a $100,000 bag of money at the end of a 20-foot 2x4 plank suspended two feet off the ground between two footings. Would you attempt to cross this plank for that kind of reward, knowing a fall might result in, at worst, a twisted ankle? Of course you would.

Now, imagine that plank elevated to fifty feet, a full five stories high. A fall from that height will mess you up big time, most likely kill you. Is the money worth the chance now?

Social Security is that bag of money waiting at the end of the plank. Most people see the process of reaching it as a relatively easy, harmless crossing and don't think twice about it. Little do they know they are actually performing a Wallenda-like endeavor that can have critical consequences on a single misstep.

---

[6] Robert Powell. MarketWatch. November 13, 2007. "True love means planning ahead." http://www.marketwatch.com/story/ten-ways-husbands-can-help-their-wives-survive-widowhood.

Decisions made regarding Social Security can last a long, long time. For the average retiree, that first decision on when to begin taking Social Security can last twenty years, often longer. For families worried about whether their savings will survive twenty to thirty years of retirement, the decision about whether to take a reduced benefit early—which the majority of people do, by the way—becomes especially meaningful when you consider that one of the two people in a couple entering retirement will live to see age eighty-five. There is a one-in-four probability that one of them will see age ninety-two.[7]

> *Two major retirement risks that all couples must plan for involve longevity, something we cannot control.*
>
> *One risk is the prospect of living too long. What if one or both members of a couple live long lives, well into their nineties or beyond? Will they be able to stretch out a retirement nest egg, should that happen? How will they cover the health care expenses that inevitably come with longer lives? What effect might inflation have in eating away at retirement savings?*
>
> *The other situation involves the loss of a spouse. Can the survivor replace the income that passes when a loved one does? How does the survivor deal with the loss of one Social Security benefit, one tax deduction, a pension payment perhaps?*
>
> *Social Security provides one of the best ways to deal with both situations. It provides income for life for two people in a couple, or the highest benefit available to one survivor. It has cost-of-living adjustments that help keep pace with inflation. These are just a few reasons why maximizing your Social Security benefit makes good sense.*

---

[7] Vanguard. "Plan for a Long Retirement."
https://personal.vanguard.com/us/insights/retirement/plan-for-a-long-retirement-tool.

For the bottom line here, let's go back to the top of this chapter.

We cited three examples, all involving people who at age sixty-six were eligible to receive the same $1,470 monthly benefit. At the age of eighty-six, the person electing to take a reduced benefit starting at age sixty-two has $317,520 (not figuring for COLAs) in total benefits after receiving twenty-four payments. The person taking his full benefit at FRA (age sixty-six) has by age eighty-six received $352,800 after twenty payments. The person deferring payments until age seventy has at age eighty-six $372,480 after only sixteen payments. His account will grow to more than $465,600 four years later if he's fortunate enough to have received twenty payments at age ninety.

When you are counting on a pool of retirement income to live longer than you do, the differences in the totals above can make a major impact on whether you achieve your goal.

CHAPTER 3

The Basics of Social Security

I f I could reduce the basics of Social Security down to its most elementary rules, I would suggest the following:

1. You've got to pay to play (or at least have a spouse who did).
2. You have to be present to win. Those who die early will receive less.
3. The longer you wait to collect, the more you stand to win.

We'll break down each of those rules in more detail shortly, but what these rules tell us in summary is this:

The amount of Social Security benefit you will ultimately receive depends on three factors. First, how long you worked and how much you paid into a system that one day will pay you back—if you are still here to collect. Which brings us to Rule Two: The total amount of your benefits depends on how long you live—a time frame none of us knows. Third, the month and year in which you begin taking benefits sets a lifetime basis for the benefit you will receive. Really, this is the only element over which we have any real control in what is an otherwise uncertain situation.

Let's also note at the start of this chapter that much of our discussion here will involve an individual's own work history benefit and how that affects other benefits to be received by a spouse or a survivor. We'll deal later with factors that determine benefits for a spouse who might not have an extensive work history, or for a surviving spouse or minor children. But let's work first on learning to add and subtract before we get into multiplication and long division.

Rule One: You've got to pay to play

You started paying for the right to play this game on the day you got your first payroll check, looked at the attached deductions stub and cried out in righteous indignation, "Who the hell is FICA, and why is he stealing part of my money?"

That's when someone older and (hopefully) wiser explained that FICA was in fact your friendly Uncle Sam and he would be withholding a part of every paycheck for as long as you work to help you save for your retirement. You, being all of sixteen years old, thought the idea of saving for retirement was just the dumbest thing you'd ever heard.

Despite such cries of youthful outrage, the Federal Insurance Contributions Act (FICA) requires you to pay 6.2 percent (under 2019 rules) of your gross pay into the Social Security trust fund, along with another 1.45 percent for Medicare. Perhaps it will cheer you up to learn your employer must match those same amounts on your behalf. (Okay, maybe that won't cheer you up.) On an even less encouraging note, self-employed people must pay withholding both as an employee and employer, meaning they lay out a full 15.3 percent in FICA taxes.

Your involuntary contributions are pooled with those of all other American workers in the Federal Old Age and Survivors

Trust Fund as well as the Federal Disability Insurance Trust Fund. The more common term for these combined pools is the Social Security Trust Fund. Managed by the Social Security Administration, the fund invests its pooled resources in securities guaranteed by the full faith and credit of the U.S. government. The fund in turn makes regular payments to seniors and persons with disabilities.

We'll talk in another chapter about the fund's solvency and long-term stability, which is another significant discussion entirely.

Within this huge fund you have your own pool of invested money. It's called your Primary Insurance Amount (PIA), and it is based on your work history and earnings. The PIA serves as the basis in computing the benefit you will receive at full retirement age, with your best thirty-five years of earnings composing that basis.

Please note: This doesn't mean you have to work thirty-five years to collect Social Security.

You *do* have to amass forty work "credits" (in SSA parlance) to be eligible for Social Security benefits. Most people earn four credits in a typical work year, meaning a ten-year employment history—though not necessarily ten consecutive years—is necessary to receive benefits.

If you work for, say, forty-plus years (as many people do before retiring), the SSA makes the top-earning thirty-five years the basis of your PIA. A work history of fewer years simply means a smaller PIA pool. The missing work years are averaged into the equation as zeros and can substantially reduce your PIA.

This is why it's not uncommon for people who have not worked that long to continue employment for slightly longer than they might have intended in order to increase their earnings pool and maximize a benefit they will receive for the rest of their lives.

Conversely, people who have worked thirty-five or more years—and I'd suggest that probably includes most people reading this book—have pretty much already topped out their PIA pool. Look at it this way: If you're reading this book at or near age sixty and you've already worked thirty-five years, you're not going to appreciably grow your PIA (and your monthly benefit) with an extra year or two of work. (We'll talk more about this in Chapter 9, about common mistakes made in Social Security.)

I encourage people—especially those wondering how much longer they might **have** to work—to track their Social Security earnings history and projected benefit, especially since it is so easy to do.

You can do this in a matter of minutes by registering your personal account at www.ssa.gov/mystatement. The secure website will take your personal information and project what your benefit—based on your earnings history at the time you make the inquiry—will be if taken at 1) the earliest possible time, 2) at full retirement age or 3) even later at age seventy.

Understanding full retirement age; the key to Social Security benefits.

It's essential here to discuss the concept of full-retirement age (FRA) as it is the key to the vast world of Social Security benefits. There are decisions to be made either before, at, or after this date that can reduce or enhance the benefits you can receive. Because of that, you absolutely **must** know your full retirement age in order to make an informed decision on when to begin taking benefits.

FRA determines, among other things, the age at which you will receive your duly-earned full benefit. It also determines how much that benefit will be reduced should you elect to begin taking benefits early—that is, in the years between age sixty-twi and your FRA. It also determines how much your enhanced benefit will be should you choose to delay taking benefits until sometime between FRA and age seventy.

It also is a key number when determining survivor and spousal benefits, both to be discussed in later chapters. FRA also is the age at which there are no restrictions on wages earned while receiving Social Security. (Restrictions are in place on wages earned when taking benefits before FRA, another topic we'll cover in more detail in Chapter 6.)

FRA has been a sliding number over its history.

When Social Security first began as a Depression Era program in the 1930s, one of its goals was to give older workers an inducement to step aside and open up jobs for younger workers desperately needing one. Age sixty-five was considered retirement age then, and a government looking for ways to create job openings did so by assuring older workers that a financial safety net would be there when they retired.

As time went on and life expectancies increased with advances in medicine and healthier lifestyles, it soon became obvious that Social Security was supporting retired people who were living longer than folks did in the 1930s.

The government consequently implemented a sliding scale that gradually increased FRA for people born between 1938 and 1942. (See the following chart) For the majority of baby boomers born from 1943 through 1954, FRA became age sixty-six. Legislation that took effect in 2000 increased the FRA to age sixty-seven for persons born in 1962 and later.

Talk continues in Congress today about further increasing the FRA as a means of Social Security reform, but sixty-seven remained the top FRA in effect in 2019.

Your Full Retirement Age			
Year of Birth	Full Retirement Age	Year of Birth	Full Retirement Age
1937 or earlier	65	1955	66 and 2 months
1938	65 and 2 months	1956	66 and 4 months
1939	65 and 4 months	1957	66 and 6 months
1940	65 and 6 months	1958	66 and 8 months
1941	65 and 8 months	1959	66 and 10 months
1942	65 and 10 months	1960 or later	67
1943—1954	66		

Rule Two: You have to be present to win

As stated at the start of this chapter, Social Security has what loosely can be called a "you have to be present to win" rule. This means— with the exception of people with disabilities—you must reach what is generally considered "retirement age" before you can start getting back the money the government has been taking from your paycheck and setting aside for you all these years.

The Social Security Administration considers this minimum age to be sixty-two. This is the soonest you can receive your personal benefits—though widows and widowers can collect slightly earlier—but sixty-two is not considered FRA. As a result, a reduced benefit is paid to persons who begin taking benefits prior to FRA on the theory that they will ultimately receive more payments over a longer period of time than will those starting benefits at FRA or later. We'll look in more detail in the next chapter at the range of reduced benefits for "early" retirees, as well as the enhanced benefits available for those who wait until after reaching FRA to begin taking benefits.

In the upcoming chapter, we'll also discuss in more detail the idea of when to begin receiving benefits. But let's just note briefly here how the prospect of not living long beyond FRA—or even getting there—weighs heavily on the minds of many people who elect to take benefits early. The idea of receiving a reduced benefit is, in the mind of many people, preferable to the prospect of receiving little or even no benefit. Moreover, the prospect of deferring benefits until age seventy, then passing shortly after that, is equally distressing. What's the use of getting an enhanced benefit, people will ask, if you only get a limited number of them?

The prospect of not living to age sixty-two is even bleaker.

For a single person who dies before reaching that age and who is without a surviving spouse or minor children, well, thanks for playing the game, as there is no prize for the late, great you. This is not a pleasant thought, but if it happens, well, you won't be around to care, will you? Nor are you likely to be consoled by the thought that your contributions to the Social Security Trust Fund are much appreciated by the people who benefited from them in the past and will do so in the future. Again, not a pleasant thought, but, as my grandfather once told me: *People make better decisions when they are brave enough to face their own mortality, and wise enough to plan accordingly.*

However, there is a consolation prize for anyone passing before full retirement age who leaves behind a surviving spouse and/or minor children. There are benefits available for surviving spouses—our entire Chapter 8 is on this subject. But even widows and widowers have to be at least age sixty (in most cases) before becoming eligible to receive survivor benefits.

There are a few significant exceptions to this rule, involving benefits available at an earlier age to surviving spouses responsible for the care of minor or disabled children. Again, we'll look at spousal and survivor benefits in more detail in later chapters.

Rule Three: The longer you wait to collect, the more you stand to win

For the vast majority of people reading this book—whom I presume to be people pondering the end of their working years and looking ahead to retirement—this is the only rule over which you have any real control at this time in your life. That alone makes this the primary reason you need to educate yourself as fully as possible about your best Social Security claiming strategy, understanding the decision you make sets the standard for the benefit you will receive for the rest of your life.

Let's be real about something here: By the time you are ready to decide when to begin taking Social Security benefits, all the other above rules have pretty much kicked in.

Rule One—"You've got to pay to play"—is largely water under the bridge. At this point in life you can't create another thirty-year work history that increases your PIA amount, the pool that determines how much benefit you will receive. What you've earned at this point in your life is pretty much all you're going to get, and even a few extra years of working isn't going to make a significant change.

Rule Two—"You must be present to win"—is about longevity and mortality, and none of us have any control over that. Let's face it, it's impossible to do any real planning over something that is completely out of our control.

Rule Three, then, is the only thing over which we now have any influence. This is where we can decide the time and the date we begin to take benefits. In doing so we also determine the size of that benefit for the remainder of our lifetime. That is, will you 1) elect to take a reduced benefit by taking Social Security before reaching FRA; 2) choose to receive your full benefit by waiting until FRA to start; or 3) opt to receive an enhanced benefit by waiting until after FRA—to as late as age seventy—to start taking benefits?

Rule Three is so important, in fact, that we will devote our entire Chapter 4 to examining the different benefit options available depending on when you initially decide to begin taking benefits.

Several more essential rules to remember

Some essential points to note here in summarizing the basics of Social Security.

One, many of the decisions you make are final when it comes to your choice of when to begin taking benefits. That's right, the benefit you receive upon first taking one stays with you for life, increasing only through cost-of-living adjustments (COLAs) made by the SSA. There are no mulligans, no do-overs except in the first year of receiving benefits (as described in the following). Moreover, the size of the benefit when first taken by a spouse affects the size of any survivor or spousal benefit that may be taken later. Again, more on this later.

There is an opportunity to change your initial election decision and reapply at a later time if done within the first twelve months of receiving payments. If executed properly, you will need to reimburse the SSA for all benefits received. This change can effectively allow you to reset your Social Security benefit options.

Such a decision will also include paying back any spousal or children's benefits received based on your benefit. You will also have to pay back any money withheld from your check for Medicare premiums or voluntary withholding tax. Make sure you seek the advice of a retirement expert or tax professional before doing this so that you can avoid critical mistakes.[8]

Two, seventy is the age at which delayed retirement credits—which grow at a rate of 8 percent annually for those waiting until after FRA to begin receiving benefits—top out. You can't increase your monthly benefit or any subsequent spousal or survivor benefit by waiting beyond age seventy to begin taking benefits.

Three, there is an income ceiling above which Social Security withholding is not taken. In 2018, any income earned above $132,900 **is not** subject to the 6.2 percent FICA withholding for Social Security. Note, however, there is no limit on income for which the 1.45 percent tax is withheld for Medicare. So, if your annual income is above $132,900 (as of 2019 rules), you will pay Social Security tax on income up to that amount, but not on income earned above it. But, you still must pay for the Medicare tax at all income levels.

Four, there is a maximum Social Security benefit that can be earned each month. In 2019, a worker retiring at FRA can receive no more than $2,861 per month. Note, however, a person waiting until after FRA to begin taking benefits will see a corresponding increase in that maximum, depending on how long he waits between FRA and age seventy to begin taking benefits.

OK, enough of the background and history lesson. Let's turn now to almost everyone's bottom line. That is, the question: At what age is it most advantageous to begin taking my Social Security benefit?

---

[8] Social Security Administration. 2018. "Retirement Planner: If You Change Your Mind."
ssa.gov/planners/retire/withdrawal.html.

I often field the question, "Am I obligated to begin taking Social Security benefits at age seventy?" The answer is no, you do not have to do so, but the reality is there is no reason not to. Your benefit will not grow through delayed retirement credits beyond age seventy. Moreover, if you don't start taking benefits until, say, age seventy-one, you've left a year of benefits just sitting on the table.

The Social Security Administration will, however, allow a person who has not taken benefits by age seventy to reclaim up to six months of previously unclaimed benefits. If you haven't taken benefits by, say, age seventy-one, you can still collect six months of the money you didn't claim, though the other six months will forever go uncollected.

Note here that this six-month "back pay" option—which is available only after reaching FRA—presents a tax strategy worth considering. Let's say a person has reached FRA and is still working. He doesn't necessarily need his Social Security benefit for immediate income. Knowing he can go back and collect six months of uncollected benefits, he might delay the start of his benefits— especially if his FRA date falls in the second half of a calendar year—until the following year. By doing so, he can take the "back pay" income in a year when he isn't working full-time, thus making it a more tax-advantageous situation. Keep in mind we are talking here about a delay of months as opposed to years.

CHAPTER 4

So, When Should I Begin Taking Social Security?

There is no right answer here, except to repeat our Rule Three stated at the top of the previous chapter. That is, the longer you wait to collect, the more you stand to receive.

This presumes you also have the good fortune to abide by the tenets of Rule Two, the one about having to be present to win. Longevity, you see, is a key component of Rule Three. This is because the total amount of benefits you get back from Uncle Sam gets bigger the longer you live. Stick around long enough and you may well get back more than the amount you paid to play. Congratulations if this happens. Conversely, Uncle's trust fund is the winner if you don't live long enough to benefit from all or most of the money you paid into the system.

Tough game, indeed.

We talked briefly in previous chapters about a key element of the game, that being the size of benefit you receive upon initially deciding whether to take a full benefit at full retirement age (FRA); a reduced benefit in a four-to-five-year window before

FRA; or an enhanced benefit in a three-to-four-year window after FRA. But let's look at this in more detail here.

In Social Security, you paid into a "pension pool" (the Social Security Trust Fund) through FICA taxes withheld from your paycheck. The SSA invests that money in government-backed securities that grow the pool of invested money.

These securities, by the way, are backed by the full faith and credit of the United States government. U.S. Treasuries, for the record, are regarded as one of the safest places to invest money by many sovereign nations around the world who invest their money here.

At the time you choose to begin taking Social Security benefits, you begin receiving a type of annuity payment for the rest of your life, not knowing whether "the rest of your life" is one day, one year, five years or thirty-plus years. As is the case with other forms of pension or annuity payments, you decide when you will begin receiving these regular monthly payments, a steady income stream once known as "mailbox income" in an era before direct deposit, when people received their Social Security checks in the mail.

Because no one knows how long you will live or how many payments you will ultimately receive, the size of each monthly benefit is determined by when you start taking benefits as well as actuary tables that project life expectancy and the number of benefits the average American is projected to receive over a lifetime.

When electing to begin taking benefits at the earliest possible time, age sixty-two, you will, in theory, be receiving more total payments than people starting at FRA (age sixty-six/sixty-seven), or even later, at age seventy. Because you are likely to receive more payments over time, the size of each payment will be smaller than the benefit you would have received if starting at FRA. Accordingly, people opting to begin benefits at an even later age will receive a greater monthly benefit based on the theory that they will receive fewer payments over their lifetime.

How much do I lose taking benefits early, or gain if I wait?

How much is the reduction for early payments, or the enhancement when starting later? Both answers depend on when you start taking benefits in relation to your all-important FRA.

Example One: A recipient with an FRA of sixty-six who begins taking benefits at age sixty-two—four years early—can see up to a 25 percent reduction in his or her monthly benefit. In monetary terms, this person's projected $2,000 benefit at FRA would be reduced to $1,500 if first taken forty-eight months early. A recipient with an even later FRA of sixty-seven who starts taking benefits at sixty-two can see up to a 30 percent reduction in benefit (reducing the monthly payment to $1,400) because he began taking benefits five years (sixty months) early.

The amount of the reduction varies inversely with the amount of time before FRA. A recipient with an FRA of sixty-six who takes benefits at age sixty-three might see only a 20 percent reduction for the thirty-six-month early window. A sixty-four-year-old with an FRA of sixty-six might see only a 13.5 percent reduction for the twenty-four-month early starting period. Again, the reduction is based on the number of months between first benefits and your FRA.

Let's look now at the upside of waiting.

People who wait until after FRA to begin taking benefits can expect to see their monthly payment increase via delayed retirement credits by 8 percent annually, or a fraction thereof depending on the number of months between FRA and the time they elect to take benefits.

Example Two: The same person described above with an FRA of sixty-six might see his projected monthly FRA benefit of $2,000 grow by 32 percent to $2,640—four years multiplied by 8 percent a year—if he delays taking benefits until age seventy. A person with an FRA of sixty-seven will see only a three-year growth of around 24 percent—three years at 8 percent—because of the reduced timeframe, but still might see his monthly benefit increased to $2,480.

One other reminder here, something we've said before but will say again because it is very, very important: The decision you make on when to receive benefits, which dictates the size of the benefit you receive, stays with you for life. There is no reset button, no stopping and starting over with a higher benefit once you've received benefits for twelve months. (This exception is the first-year benefits "pay back" option we discussed in Chapter 3.) The SSA will occasionally increase a benefit through cost-of-living adjustments (COLAs, which we will discuss in more detail later in this chapter), but there is no second chance, should you come to regret the all-important decision you made initially.

See the big picture: Breakeven points don't tell the whole story

I discussed elsewhere the need to see "the big picture" when it comes to Social Security benefits. In short, that means looking at the total amount of benefits one might expect to receive at various points of life expectancy when those benefits are first taken before, at, or after FRA.

Many clients attempting a big-picture look come into my office with nice-looking spreadsheets or charts projecting total benefits when first taken at different ages in retirement. Their graphs usually have three different lines: One depicting benefits when first taken at age sixty-two, another projecting benefits when first taken at age sixty-six, and a third with benefits first taken at age seventy.

Their charts often look like the following.

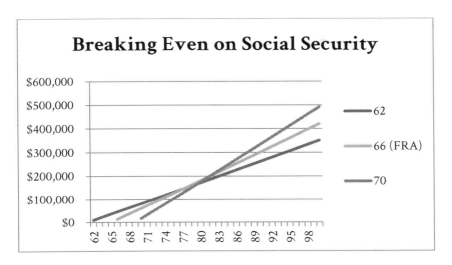

A chart like this is a nice start, but that is all it is.

The darkest line depicts total benefits received—with dollar amounts shown on the vertical axis and age displayed on the horizontal—when first taken early, in this case at age sixty-two. The lightest line shows total benefits when first taken at FRA, age sixty-six in the above chart. The medium line depicts total benefits when first taken later at age seventy.

You can see the three lines intersecting somewhere around age eighty, which is a reasonably accurate projection of the age at which total benefits received become equal whether taken early, or at FRA, or on a deferred basis.

You can see how a person taking benefits at age seventy will be leaving money on the table—compared to his counterparts in the early retirement and full retirement categories—if he leaves us too many years before age eighty. Conversely, you also can see where our patient friend starts to pull ahead of the field around age eighty-five, then takes a big lead in total benefits received if he lives to age ninety and beyond.

Consider the effect of taxes, cost-of-living adjustments

This chart serves a purpose, but it still doesn't tell the full story of other factors you need to consider if your goal is to maximize your Social Security benefits as a means of increasing your total retirement nest egg.

The first factor to consider is the effect of taxes.

We'll discuss more extensively in Chapter 5 the effects of Social Security on taxes in retirement. But for now, let's just note in passing that taxes on Social Security benefits are considerably less than those on fully taxed income taken from qualified retirement accounts such as 401(k)s and IRAs. Moreover, for persons with a yearly income below a certain level, there is no tax at all on Social Security benefits.

According to rules in place in 2019, no more than 85 percent of an annual Social Security benefit can be taxed, should the benefit recipient have a provisional income—which we will define in Chapter 5—above $34,000 for a single-filer return, or $44,000 for a joint return. The maximum taxable amount of an annual benefit drops to 50 percent if your provisional income is between $25,000 and $34,000 for a single filer, or between $32,000 and $44,000 for a joint return. Better yet, your Social Security benefits are not taxed at all if your provisional income is below $25,000 for a single filer and $32,000 on a joint return.

Second, consider the effects of cost-of-living adjustments on your "big picture."

Annual COLAs made by the SSA during recent years of relatively low inflation haven't been as generous as they were years ago in times of greater inflation, which only makes sense. Still, COLAs can add up to a significant number over a long period of time, especially when applied to a larger benefit, so let's not overlook their value.

Keep in mind, retirement income planning comes down to cash flow, and any increase in monthly cash flow is helpful. But that increase becomes even more significant when factoring in the base amount being increased.

Consider the hypothetical $2,000 monthly benefit of the recipient described earlier in this chapter who started taking benefits at FRA (age sixty-six). After one year, he gets a 2 percent COLA—the amount approved for 2018, a huge hike over 2017 when the COLA was only 0.3 percent—giving him an additional $40 each month. OK, he might spend all of that in one place, but it's still a $480 annual increase that hikes his Year Two annual benefit from $24,000 to $24,480. That increased benefit now serves as the new basis that will grow with future COLAs. Keep in mind, for 2019, the annual COLA amount has been ap-proved for 2.8 percent, the largest annual increase since 2012.

Now consider his same-age buddy cited above in Example One, the guy whose projected $2,000 monthly benefit was reduced to $1,500 because he began taking benefits four years earlier at age sixty-two.

Let's say he gets the same 2 percent COLA on his initial annual benefit of $18,000 in each of those four years. His monthly benefit at the end of four years (when he is sixty-six) has risen only to $1,623, and his annual benefit has risen to only $19,483—considerably below that of his friend who started taking benefits at FRA and is now receiving a $24,480 annual benefit after only one year of benefits and one COLA.

The third member of our same-age triad (Example Two) who deferred benefits for four years to age seventy will fare even better. With a 2 percent COLA after one year, he sees his $2,640 initial monthly benefit rise by $52 per month and $633 annually. At age seventy-one, after only one year of benefits and one COLA, his annual benefit has risen from $31,680 to $32,313, and it is only going to grow from there with each additional COLA.

Bottom line, all Social Security beneficiaries receive the same COLA increase, but that increase means more money every month for those with a bigger base to grow. That is, those who waited until FRA or later to begin taking benefits.

Finally, consider the value of delayed retirement credits strictly as an investment.

For people who have means to wait until age seventy before taking benefits, your PIA pool is growing at 8 percent a year until it stops growing at age seventy. Think of that pool as an investment. How many at-risk, market-based investments do you know that are guaranteed by the good faith and credit of the U.S. government to grow at 8 percent a year in both up markets and down ones?

Is the mathematical optimum the best choice for you?

Okay, I know what is coming next. You have every reason to say, "You still haven't answered my initial question. When is the best time to begin taking Social Security benefits?"

Well, as we discussed at the beginning of this chapter, the question is highly subjective. The point to be emphasized here is there is no one set answer that works for everyone when it comes to determining the "optimal" time to begin taking Social Security. This is because while "optimal" Social Security planning is one thing, what may be optimal in your special situation might be something completely different. The challenge facing you and the advisor with whom you are working is to determine what works best for you and your family. Just make sure you understand all the implications of your decision before you make it.

Clearly, the bottom line is that people who can wait until full retirement age, whether sixty-six or sixty-seven or somewhere in between, will receive a bigger monthly benefit and a potentially bigger pool of lifetime benefits—depending on longevity—than will people who begin taking benefits at age sixty-two or any other time prior to reaching FRA.

Beyond that, we've demonstrated that a person with the will and means to wait until age seventy—be it a willingness to continue working to that point or having other financial resources from which to draw retirement income while waiting to collect Social Security—will receive a considerably bigger monthly benefit than either our early recipient or an FRA recipient. Moreover, the person waiting until age seventy will have a considerably bigger pool of total benefits if he has the good fortune to live longer than age eighty.

But the question of which strategy is best for you—taking a reduced benefit early, a full benefit at FRA or an enhanced benefit after FRA—depends on how you analyze your own personal situation.

A real-life illustration here.

I once had a sixty-eight-year-old client with a goal of delaying Social Security until age seventy for all the reasons you now understand. But he'd had some misfortune earlier in life when, through no fault of his own, he underwent several years of unemployment. He'd tapped into a bunch of his retirement savings during that time, knowing it wasn't the smart thing to do, but also knowing he had to put food on his family's table and keep the lights turned on. Consequently, at age sixty-eight, his retirement resources weren't what they needed to be, so he came to me wondering whether he could wait another two years before taking his maximum enhanced benefit.

> *Well, sure, I could easily have shown him mathematically how waiting another two years would be financially beneficial in the long run. But the reality of this man's life was that taking Social Security benefits at sity-eight put him in a better position to help his family now, which was his most pressing need. Did he make a mistake by taking benefits two years earlier than the computer software and financial models might suggest? Not necessarily.*

Admittedly, for people with chronic disease or a family history that does not include longevity, the prospect of taking benefits early makes some sense. The idea of "get what I can while I can" is not without merit for many people.

Moreover, other people have simply had enough of the workaday world after forty-plus years and look forward to an early retirement. Many calculate they can live a reasonable lifestyle on a reduced Social Security benefit that is supplemented with 401(k) or IRA income, coupled with mailbox income from an annuity or pension. If necessary, they accept the prospect of part-time work as a means of supplementing income, as well as providing a meaningful way to spend retirement days.

Good for those who are comfortable with that choice.

It's easier to prepare for the future when you've planned in the past

The decision you make about when to begin taking benefits will depend on any number of factors, but one factor jumps out at the start.

People who have been diligent in their working years about saving and investing and looking ahead to retirement—a group that includes most readers of this book, I strongly suspect—generally have resources available that allow them to be more proactive in the Social Security decisions they make, decisions that have the potential to produce a larger pool of benefits for those with longevity on their side.

Such people might, for example, be able to retire early, yet delay taking Social Security benefits until a later, more income-beneficial time. They do this knowing they have other retirement resources they can use for income as they bridge the gap between the time they stop working and the time they begin taking benefits at FRA or later. They are fully prepared to draw down their qualified IRA accounts or non-qualified brokerage accounts today in the knowledge they are likely to receive a lifelong enhanced Social Security benefit later.

These people with the foresight to save and invest during their working years are the fortunate ones. Too many other people, sadly, do not have a reservoir of other retirement assets, leaving Social Security as their principal source of retirement income.

For them, the best available option might well be to continue working for as long as they can—at least to FRA, if not longer. By working to FRA they can 1) receive the full benefit to which they are due, and 2) effectively "double dip," meaning they continue to work while receiving Social Security benefits. As we will discuss in more detail in our Chapter 6 on working while receiving benefits, there is no limit to the amount of wages you can earn without penalty after a worker reaches FRA.

Keep in mind here, there is nothing written in stone that says you absolutely MUST start taking Social Security immediately after you leave the workaday world. This is a popular concept, but it doesn't work for everyone. Some people will continue to work because they HAVE to, others because they WANT to. Just keep in mind that, as we will discuss in Chapter 6, people who take benefits prior to their FRA face a penalty for wages earned above a certain limit—another reason for delaying benefits until FRA or even later. In addition, benefits taken after full retirement age are no longer subjected to the wage-earning test.

It's been said that financial planning often involves making an informed decision about an uncertain future. We make decisions today that could impact us over thirty years of retirement, knowing as we do so, it is impossible to know what those next thirty years will look like or even if we will have that time available. Yet, we make those decisions nonetheless based on the best information available to us today.

This is why it is important to go through this exercise with a professional who asks the right questions, who can help steer you into making decisions that can work for you based on the information available to you now.

This must be somebody with your best interests at heart, someone interested in more than selling investment products. It must be somebody with a strong understanding of your current financial situation as well as your future retirement goals. Someone who helps you see how taxes, inflation, and the need to finance long-term care fit into the big picture that is your retirement.

It's only my personal opinion—though it is based on years of experience—that your professional advisor also should be someone who fully understands the rules and complexities of Social Security. Sadly, not all advisors can say that. Yet, Social Security remains the biggest piece of the retirement puzzle for most retirees, and as such it simply has to work most efficiently to properly complement all the other pieces you've spent a lifetime of hard work compiling.

CHAPTER 5

Taxes and Social Security

I can almost hear your question before you ask it.

Social Security benefits are taxable? You gotta be kidding me. I mean, didn't I already pay a Social Security tax during all those years when I was working? It hardly seems fair that to get taxed again when I start receiving benefits I essentially paid for.

Well, the good news is that not everyone will pay tax on their Social Security benefits, though a majority of benefit recipients will.[9] [10]

It all depends on how much ***provisional income***—a concept explained elsewhere in this chapter—an individual or couple made in the previous year. If your combined income is below certain levels, which is the case for many people receiving Social Security as their primary source of retirement income, you may owe no tax at all on the benefits you receive. The bad news is, if you make above a certain limit—common among people with other income from

---

[9] In 2015 the Social Security Administration projected that 56 percent of beneficiary families would pay taxes on parts of their Social Security benefits between 2015 and 2050.

[10] Patrick J. Purcell. Social Security Administration. December 2015. https://papers.ssrn.com/sol3/papers.cfm?abstract_id=2702427.

stock and bond dividends, interest, rentals, pensions, or other income sources—you may owe tax on up to a maximum of 85 percent of your benefits.

Social Security benefits weren't always taxable, mind you.

When President Franklin Roosevelt established Social Security in 1935 as a New Deal program designed to address rampant double-digit unemployment during the Great Depression, Social Security benefits were not taxed. Pensions were—for the most part—non-existent then, and people in their sixties could hardly afford to leave their jobs voluntarily.

To deal with that reality, Social Security was created as a kind of national pension system. (It later also became a social insurance program to help people with disabilities.) As a pension program, workers ponied up part of their weekly paycheck to pay for the retirement of people in or near retirement age, as well as for the retirement of future generations. The promise was that someday those benefits would be there for them when it came time for their retirement. Not everyone liked that idea at the time—some still don't even today—so FDR had to sweeten the pot by promising to never tax that retirement income.

What are some tax-planning strategies, and why aren't I hearing more about them?

We talked earlier in this chapter about how taxes are often the second-biggest drain on retirement nest eggs, typically trailing only health care. Knowing this to be the case, it only makes sense to make tax-planning strategies an essential part of any retirement plan.

Sadly, too many financial advisors fail to do this with their clients. And some of the reason for that has to do with the nature of the business.

Let's explain this by first asking a question. Which is the better source of income: $1,000 taken from a tax-deferred IRA or 401(k), or $1,000 taken from Social Security? The answer is, the Social Security money on which a maximum of 85 percent might be taxed will yield more after-tax income than any IRA distribution, 100 percent of which is taxed as regular income.

This brings up a situation many people face going into retirement, or at the point where they decide when to begin taking Social Security. The question they face is: Is it more tax advantageous to take Social Security income first while letting IRA accounts grow, or to take income from IRA accounts first while letting future Social Security benefits grow?

I would answer that by reminding you, once again, at least 15 percent (and possibly more) of your Social Security benefits are tax-free under the laws in place in 2017. Not even Warren Buffett will pay tax on more than 85 percent of his benefits.

Let's look at some numbers. A $3,000 monthly benefit check taken beginning at age seventy will have at least $450 (15 percent) of tax-free money. An $1,800 benefit check—which the above benefit might have been reduced to if taken at age sixty-two—will have up to only $270 guaranteed as tax free. (Another reason for delaying the start of benefits until age seventy if at all possible.)

Knowing this, why wouldn't you want to expand the more tax-efficient income base—i.e., grow your Social Security account—that is at least 15 percent tax free? I would suggest using fully taxable IRA money—which you're going to pay tax on eventually, whether now or when RMDs kick in at age seventy-and-one-half—as your income bridge to an enhanced Social Security benefit. This is certainly preferable to taking a reduced Social Security benefit—one that permanently reduces your base of potential tax-beneficial income—in order to continue growing qualified accounts upon which you will be fully taxed at some time. Talk about kicking the can down the road!

Conventional wisdom would have retirees withdraw or sell investments held in fully taxable accounts—such as non-qualified brokerage accounts—before touching the money in their tax-deferred accounts such as IRAs, 401(k)s, or qualified annuities. Doing so, however, could cost you more in tax liability and create a bigger drain on your after-tax wealth. Tax laws tend to have a long-term view on retirement savings accounts, which means you likewise should take the same long-term view.

I hope to further illustrate in the next section of this chapter why I believe the second of the above two options—that is, deferring the start of Social Security benefits while drawing early income from IRA accounts—is preferable.

Again, you won't always get this advice from all financial advisors or your mutual fund provider. It's not in their interest, frankly, to take this approach. That's because part of what they get paid is based on "money under management," so it makes sense that they are not especially eager to see you drain your IRA as a bridge to getting to enhanced Social Security benefits.

Moreover, because the fee structure for doing Roth conversions is not lucrative and tends to create uncomfortable discussions at tax time for most brokers/advisors, many don't push the long-term benefits of moving money from tax-deferred IRAs into Roth accounts from which distributions can be taken by you (or your heirs/beneficiaries after you pass) on a tax-free basis.

One last editorial comment here. The failure of too many brokers/advisors to give advice that might be in the best interest of a client, but not necessarily in their best interest, is a pet peeve of mine. Sometimes you truly have to ask: Are you getting a biased assessment from the financial industry because of how they get paid?

No good deed goes unpunished

Changes in Social Security are always evolving.

I was just a pre-teen in the late 1970s when I first remember hearing people worry about the long-term sustainability of Social Security. Many of these people, mind you, were members of "The Greatest Generation," the men and women who were there for their country in World War II, but now wondered if their country's retirement program would be there for them.

Needless to say, I was too young then to fully comprehend what my parents and national leaders such as President Jimmy Carter were worrying about. What I did know was that this was a time of gasoline shortages and long lines at the pumps. I see it today as a time of uncertainty shortly after the end of the controversial Vietnam War, when Americans started questioning whether we could maintain our high standard of living as well as the social safety nets we had come to take for granted.

Looking back today at a period Carter once described as a "national malaise," I can see where baby boomers older than myself first began to share concerns voiced by their parents that the Social Security system into which they'd been paying for years might not be there for them when it came their turn to retire. Such concerns remain alive even today, and expressing my personal belief that some form of Social Security will be around for generations to come does little to alleviate such concerns. That's especially the case for people who take Social Security benefits at the first opportunity, doing so on the "get it while you can" theory.

Seeking to do something to maintain the long-term solvency of the Social Security system, in 1983 President Ronald Reagan signed legislation establishing the first tax on Social Security benefits.

It was described then as a tax on the rich, people with combined income—also known as "provisional income"—of more than

$25,000 as an individual or $32,000 as a couple. An individual or couple with provisional income above those levels might have up to 50 percent of their Social Security benefits subject to tax. Conversely, an individual or couple with provisional income under $25,000 or $32,000, respectively, would pay no tax on their benefits.

In 1993 Congress decided it hadn't gone far enough and a new Social Security tax bracket was established under President Bill Clinton. Now, in addition to the 50 percent income levels established in 1983, an individual with more than $34,000 in provisional income or a couple with more than $44,000 could see up to 85 percent of their Social Security benefits subject to tax. Those limits are still in place today.

> *Note the 50 and 85 percent figures mentioned above do not mean Social Security benefits are taxed at 50 or 85 percent rates; that is, you do not pay an 85 percent tax rate on your benefits.*
>
> *Rather, those figures represent how much of your benefits might be taxed at your normal tax rate, which is based on how much you make in taxable income.*

Well, American wages and earning power has increased considerably since the establishment of income thresholds in 1983 and 1993. Consequently, people we would hardly consider "rich" by today's standards find themselves paying taxes on their Social Security benefits.

As taxes represent one of the biggest drains on retirement savings, it is important to be aware of Social Security taxes and to develop retirement plans that take these taxes into consideration. Legally minimizing your tax liability through tax-efficient investment and withdrawal strategies can mean keeping more of your retirement nest egg. As I tell my clients frequently, it's not what you earn in life but how much you keep that is most important in retirement planning. A comprehensive retirement plan simply must include a consideration of how to tactically plan for taxes.

Moreover, it is equally important to keep an eye on possible future changes in the Social Security tax structure, such as the possibility that 100 percent of Social Security benefits may someday be taxed. If you are reading this book in 2018, you might well be in a group that someday will have to pay that. You need to start planning with an expert now to adjust for this possibility.

Any discussion about how Social Security might change in the future necessarily merits a quick mention of how it has changed in the past.

The Social Security program of 2018 is different from what your grandparents and even your parents likely knew. In the 1950s and '60s, for instance, Social Security along with a work pension and a small amount of savings was expected to pretty much provide all the retirement income a couple might need. Remember, too, that prior to 1983, Social Security was a tax-free source of income and therefore provided a large pool of income. People didn't live as long back then, either, so taking benefits at age sixty-two didn't carry as big a chance of leaving benefits on the table as it does today when people routinely live into their 90s. Moreover, there once was a time when you couldn't work while collecting Social Security early at age sixty-two.

Many of those situations have changed today, especially the part about being able to work while collecting benefits. On the downside, work-sponsored pension programs have given way to self-funded 401(k)s, meaning guaranteed pensions are disappearing from the picture while market-based savings programs are becoming a big factor. Social Security alone probably won't fund all your retirement income needs.

How is provisional income determined?

Let's take a quick couple of minutes here and detail how one determines how much of their Social Security benefits—if any—will be taxed.

Again, that amount is determined by an individual's or couple's combined income, also called provisional income or "modified adjusted gross income" (MAGI).

Here is how that figure is determined.

MAGI includes all components that go into figuring your adjusted gross income (AGI) on your tax return. This includes all your income from wages; self-employment income; taxable interest: ordinary dividends from stocks and bonds; capital gains; the taxable amount of distributions from IRAs, pensions, or annuities; alimony received; and income from rentals, royalties, trusts, and farming.

And we're not done with the addition part just yet.

Remember how the broker who sold you municipal bonds, or shares in a municipal bond mutual fund, promoted such investments by saying they were not taxed on your federal return? Such a statement is not entirely wrong, but it's also not completely right. That's because income from tax-exempt municipal bonds (line 8B on the 2016 IRS Form 1040) *is* a component of provisional income and is added onto the total income number.

Now comes yet another rather significant addition.

One half of your total Social Security benefit—paid either as an individual or a couple—also is added to the total.

You now have your MAGI, or provisional income figure.

It may sound complicated—and you should consult with a tax professional if you require additional help, which some people do—but you are basically plugging in numbers you entered on Form 1040. Tax software programs will do this calculation to determine whether you owe any—or how much—tax on your benefits. Any tax owed on Social Security benefits is entered as regular income on line 20b of Form 1040.

Let's repeat something here.

Many people receiving Social Security benefits, especially those for whom Social Security is their only significant source of income, will pay no tax at all on their benefits.

But for those with other income sources—part-time work, investment dividends, pension or annuity payments, required minimum distributions (RMDs) from IRA accounts, rental property income, municipal bond income and other sources—it's not difficult to exceed the thresholds into the 50 or even 85 percent Social Security income levels.

And for that prospect you should plan to plan accordingly.

Twin brothers, different strategies, different results

Once upon a time there were twin brothers.

No, this isn't the start of a fairy tale or off-color joke. Rather, it is a way to illustrate how income-producing approaches and tax strategies can have a vastly different impact on two people in the same situation.

Both men were solid producers in life with a combination of retirement accounts and assets such that they could comfortably retire at age sixty-two. Both decide they will need $60,000 annually to live the retirement lifestyle of their choosing.

Bob elects to take Social Security at his earliest opportunity—age sixty-two, and will receive a benefit in this example of $20,000 a year for the rest of his life, not counting cost-of-living adjustments. He will fill his annual income goal by taking $40,000 out of his IRA, annuities, or other fully taxable retirement accounts.

Larry, on the other hand, chooses to delay receiving Social Security benefits until age seventy. His benefits grow over eight years through delayed credits and cost-of-living adjustments until he is entitled to receive a benefit of nearly $40,000 (rounded up slightly for the purpose of convenient illustration). He will meet the rest of his $60,000 annual income goal by taking only $20,000 from his IRA accounts for the rest of his life.

The following chart shows the tax effect on the two men in the first year of Larry taking benefits—the eighth such year for Bob.

Larry vs. Bob		
	Larry	Bob
	Year 1	Year 8
	Both are 70 Years Old	
Gross IRA Income	$20,000	$40,000
Gross Social Security	$40,000	$20,000
Gross Income	$60,000	$60,000
Percent of Social Security Subject to Tax	10%	56%
Taxable Social Security Benefit	$4,000	$11,100
Adjusted Gross Income	$24,000	$51,100
Exemptions/ Deductions	$26,600	$26,600
Total Taxable Income	--	$24,500
Effective Tax Rate	--	10.46%
Federal Tax	--	$2,562
State Tax	--	$1,214
Total Taxes	--	$3,776
After-Tax Income	$60,000	$56,224

Because Bob is being taxed on all of the $40,000 annual distribution from his qualified retirement accounts, his provisional income is at such a level that more than 50 percent of his Social Security benefits are taxable. With $11,100 in taxable Social Security benefits, his adjusted gross income (AGI) in this example is $51,100. After taking $26,600 in exemptions and standard deductions for himself and his wife (as they are filing jointly), his taxable income is $24,500, which puts him in the 12 percent tax bracket (under 2019 tax codes). Bob might expect to pay around $3,776 in taxes on that amount—again, based on tax rates in effect in 2019.

Now we look at Larry's tax situation in that same year.

Because he's now paying full taxes on only $20,000 of IRA distributions, Larry finds only 10 percent of the $40,000 he received in first-year Social Security benefits are taxable. With only $4,000 of taxable Social Security income, Larry's AGI is $24,000 (compared to Bob's $51,100). After taking the same $26,600 in standard deductions and exemptions as did Brother Bob, Larry and his wife have taxable income of $0. Their total tax bill in their first year of taking Social Security benefits is a big old goose egg.

Admittedly, reading only the bottom line—Bob's tax bill of $3,776 compared to Larry's $0—is unfair without some nuance. For people who really like to break down the numbers—and I deal with a lot of engineers and mathematicians who do—let's note we did not include in this example other sources of taxable income such as dividends, capital gains, and part-time wages the two successful businessmen would likely realize in retirement. This example serves mainly to illustrate the difference in taxes when taking a bigger share of retirement income from Social Security as opposed to tax-deferred accounts such as IRAs.

Beyond that, many numbers crunchers also will note correctly, while Larry has been waiting eight years to grow his Social Security benefit, he also has been draining his IRA resources—and paying taxes on—$60,000 a year, or $480,000 total ($60,000 multiplied by eight) between ages sixty-two and seventy. (Remember, we said both these guys were good earners and savers.) Bob, in those same eight years, has taken only $320,000 ($40,000 multiplied by eight) from his IRA resources.

Now, let's look at the total drain on IRA resources when we extend our projection to when the twins reach age eighty.

Bob's IRA resources have now been depleted by eighteen years (from age sixty-two to eighty) of withdrawals of $40,000 annually, a pre-tax total of $720,000. Keep in mind he also will pay 12 to 15 percent of that amount—another $108,000, say—for taxes.

Larry drained his IRA resources by $480,000 for the first eight years—after retiring at sixty-two until taking Social Security at age seventy), but only $200,000 in the following decade ($20,000 annually for ten years). The total drain on his IRA resources after eighteen years is $680,000—about $40,000 under that of his twin. Moreover, because Larry started receiving more tax-advantageous Social Security money at age seventy, he is employing a tax strategy that reduces the amount of fully taxable IRA money he is taking—from $60,000 to $20,000—in the final ten years of this eighteen-year example. By better managing his tax liability, Larry is likely after eight years to still be paying next to nothing, or, given that the current tax code is set to "sunset" in 2025, he may be in a 10 percent bracket. Regardless, the low tax situation is one that will save him considerable money.

Damn the torpedo taxes

In our working years before the idea of receiving Social Security loomed, we somewhat eagerly accepted the idea that significant increases in income—whether through promotions or new jobs or lucrative new projects—meant we might well be kicked up into a higher tax bracket. We took the extra money as it came and worried about taxes only in April.

Upon receiving Social Security benefits, however, we suddenly face a potential double whammy when looking at the otherwise pleasant prospect of increased income.

This happens when the chance of being elevated into a higher tax bracket—one of the last things you want in retirement—is increased by the effect of rising provisional income on Social Security taxation. Believe it or not, incomes can and do increase considerably in retirement, especially after age seventy-and-one-half when everyone has to start taking RMDs from tax-deferred accounts upon which we've paid no tax all these years. What, you didn't think Uncle Sam would demand his cut eventually?

Keep in mind, too, that these distributions you are required to take (whether you want/need them or not) only increase in size every year after age seventy-and-one-half. (Uncle is really, really determined to get his full share before you leave him.) What that means for individuals with more than $32,000 in annual provisional income, and couples filing jointly with more than $44,000, is that each additional $1 in income effectively creates an additional $1.85 of taxable income when 85 percent of Social Security benefits are subject to taxation.

I (and others) call this the "torpedo tax," a term for taxes many people don't see coming until they get hit amidships.

And these taxes do hit hard. Not only are you paying regular income tax on the additional RMD money you must take each year, you could well find yourself in a higher tax bracket when additional taxable income from Social Security is factored in.

Let's call on our friend Larry from the previous example for an illustration of what can happen when he gets torpedoed. To recap, Larry is the guy who delayed taking his Social Security benefits until they reached their highest possible level at age seventy. At this point he was meeting his $60,000 annual income goal with (roughly) $40,000 in Social Security and only $20,000 from his IRA resources. Recall his adjusted gross income at these levels was $24,000—the full $20,000 from the IRA, but only $4,000 (10 percent of the $40,000) taxable from Social Security. After exemptions and deductions, he was paying nothing in taxes.

A year later, Larry is seventy-one and has to start taking $10,000 in RMDs from his IRA accounts. Or, perhaps he needs an additional $10,000 for a health emergency, a home repair or his wife's dream trip to Europe. Whatever the case, his IRA distribution rises from $20,000 to $30,000. Let's look at what that does to his tax situation in the following chart.

Larry, Before and After RMDs		
	Year 1	Year 2
Gross IRA Income	$20,000	$30,000
Gross Social Security	$40,000	$40,000
Gross Income	$60,000	$70,000
Percent of Social Security Subject to Tax	10%	28%
Taxable Social Security Benefit	$4,000	$11,100
Adjusted Gross Income	$24,000	$41,100
Exemptions/ Deductions	$26,600	$26,600
Total Taxable Income	--	$14,500
Effective Tax Rate	--	10.02%
Federal Tax	--	$1,453
State Tax	--	$679
Total Taxes	--	$2,132
After-Tax Income	*$60,000*	*$67,868*

Not only does the full $30,000 become part of his AGI, but so does $11,100 of his Social Security benefits—28 percent of $40,000. His AGI in one year rises from $24,000 to $41,100 and his taxable income goes from $0 to $14,500. He's fortunate to remain in the 10 percent tax bracket after exemptions and deductions, but his tax bill rises nonetheless from $0 to $2,132 in one year.

Brother Bob is in even worse shape, according to his chart.

Bob, Before and After RMDs		
	Year 8	**Year 9**
Gross IRA Income	$40,000	$50,000
Gross Social Security	$20,000	$20,000
Gross Income	$60,000	$70,000
Percent of Social Security Subject to Tax	56%	85%
Taxable Social Security Benefit	$11,100	$17,000
Adjusted Gross Income	$51,100	$67,000
Exemptions/ Deductions	$26,600	$26,600
Total Taxable Income	$24,500	$40,400
Effective Tax Rate	10.46%	11.06%
Federal Tax	$2,562	$4,470
State Tax	$1,214	$2,078
Total Taxes	$3,766	$6,548
After-Tax Income	*$56,234*	*$63,452*

Bob, you may remember, took Social Security early, taking a $20,000 annual benefit and $40,000 from his IRA to meet his

$60,000 annual income goal. Now, at age seventy-one, he finds himself taking an additional $10,000 in IRA resources (same as brother Larry), either voluntarily or because of RMDs. Now he is paying tax on the full $50,000 from his IRA, and his provisional income has increased to the point that he is paying tax on the maximum 85 percent of his Social Security benefit—$17,000 of taxable income compared to $11,100 before he was "torpedoed." After exemptions and deductions his taxable income rises from $24,500 to $40,400, and even though he remains in the 12 percent tax bracket, his tax bill rises from $3,766 to $6,548 in one year.

Bottom line for the brothers: After both realized a $10,000 hike in income because of RMDs at age seventy-one, Larry's after-tax income picture improved by $7,868, rising from $60,000 at age seventy to $67,868 one year later. Bob's $10,000 hike in income produced only a $7,218 after-tax bump, and his annual income rose from $56,234 at age seventy to $63,452 a year later—$5,000 behind his twin who waited to age seventy to begin taking Social Security benefits.

An important point to remember when considering comprehensive retirement planning advice: It's not what you get but what you get to keep that counts most. Make sure you consider tax planning before making your financial planning decisions. (A topic for my next book perhaps.)

The importance of proper planning

The ultimate point to be made here is that real retirement planning involves far more than making good investments or understanding the breakeven points at which Social Security payouts become equal whether started at age sixty-two, at full retirement age, or at age seventy.

It simply is not enough to work with someone selling you products and investments. You need an advisor who looks at everything comprehensively, who can detail how all the puzzle pieces fit together in your retirement picture.

An advisor who doesn't talk with you about the implication of taxes in retirement—and especially about how Social Security taxes can affect your overall tax bill—isn't giving you the full picture. Many advisors will touch on the importance of maximizing Social Security, but don't provide nearly enough detail on how to do it. Limiting your tax liability is a big component of any maximization strategy—and we'll talk about some others in following chapters—but I see new clients frequently who tell me their advisor has said little about filling tax-advantageous buckets such as the Roth IRA, or the tax implications of taking Social Security benefits later as opposed to earlier.

It's also important to have an advisor with some vision on where Social Security may go in the near future. I'll repeat here my belief that it will be around for years to come, but changes may well be coming with new political administrations and new ideas of what needs to be done to "save" Social Security.

CHAPTER 6

Working While Taking
Social Security Benefits

The concept of "retirement" can mean different things to different people.

For the definitive word on the subject we turn to the Merriam-Webster dictionary where we find retirement defined in part as "withdrawal from one's position or occupation, or from active working life." That pretty well sums it up, especially in the key words "from active working life."

I say this only because anyone who thinks "retirement" means the end of one's working days is kidding themselves.

Let's be honest here: There is always work to be done in retirement. It could be work you've been putting off on your home or other property. It might be work for which your children need a helping hand, or work with a charitable organization. Maybe it's part-time work in an occupation for which you still have some affinity, or work in a field different than what you knew during all your years in the workaday world.

People work after "retirement" for any number of reasons. Many need the cash flow to supplement what they receive from Social Security and other retirement savings. Many work to pay off debt or fund a dream vacation. Some work to complete professional goals they didn't achieve before reaching "retirement age." Others work simply for the fulfillment of doing so, to keep themselves occupied and to fight off boredom.

Whatever your reason for choosing to work in retirement, whether in a paid capacity or otherwise, the key is being able to work on your own terms, or terms mutually acceptable to you and an employer. Retirement should mean you are now in control of how much or how little you choose to work, with "choose" being the operative word. Or such is the ideal.

In making that choice for yourself, however, it also is important to understand how wages earned in retirement can affect your Social Security benefit.

Earnings limits can affect benefits

Let's deal with some good news first.

That is, upon reaching your full retirement age—that sliding FRA number between sixty-six and sixty-seven that we defined in previous chapters—the Social Security Administration (SSA) places no limit on the amount of wages you can earn while receiving Social Security benefits. That's right, at FRA you have the opportunity to do some true double-dipping when it comes to receiving your full benefit at the same time you are earning as much in wage income as you choose to pursue.

When we talk about the advantages of waiting until FRA to begin taking benefits, this aspect alone is an important consideration.

That's especially true when we consider the penalty on those who earn too much in wage income while taking Social Security benefits before reaching FRA.

Under the rules in place in 2019, the SSA is required to take back $1 in benefits for every $2 you earn in wages above an earnings limit of $17,640—a limit that generally increases each year. Again, this is a reduction in benefits only to people taking Social Security before reaching FRA.

Fortunately, that earnings limit eases considerably as you near FRA.

Starting in January of the year in which you reach FRA, the earnings limit (in 2019) rises to $46,920. The amount of benefit reduction also is lowered to $1 taken back for every $3 earned over the limit. The earnings limit is completely eliminated beginning in the month you reach FRA.

Let's look at an example of how this might work.

Consider a sixty-three-year-old "retiree" who began taking Social Security benefits a year earlier at the earliest possible opportunity, age sixty-two. His/her normal monthly benefit is $1,000, and the annual benefit $12,000. In 2019, he/she continued to work on a limited basis and received $21,640 in wages, $4,000 more than the 2018 earnings limit of $17,640.

Consequently, the SSA will take back $1 in benefits for every $2 earned above the limit, or $2,000 total ($4,000 divided by two). His/her total annual benefit in 2019 will be reduced by that amount to $10,000. The SSA will meet the $2,000 "take back" by not paying the $1,000 monthly benefit for two months.

But, upon reaching full retirement age, the SSA will adjust his/her benefit to restore the benefits taken in 2019 and any other years in which the earnings limit was exceeded.

As noted above, when the SSA learns it needs to "take back" benefit money because of excessive wage earnings, it does so by withholding benefit checks until the "take back" amount is realized. Typically, this happens after you file your taxes for, say, 2018 in the spring of 2019. The SSA, upon seeing that you earned too much in wages in '18, might start withholding checks in the summer or fall of 2019, which can produce some budgeting problems when you're suddenly not getting monthly income you were expecting.

The best way to deal with such a situation is to advise the SSA as soon as you suspect you will exceed the wage limits. You can make it administratively easier on yourself when you can voluntarily report the situation and plan on a temporary benefit stoppage than it is when the SSA catches it and stops payments when you least expect it.

Special rules of note

Let's note some other essential points here before we discuss the idea of whether or not it is advisable to limit wage income while taking Social Security benefits.

First, benefits taken back because of excessive income earned before reaching FRA are not forever lost. As noted above, the SSA will gradually restore any benefit previously taken by increasing your benefit once you reach FRA. In effect, the pay cut you may have taken when working from age sixty-two through sixty-six/sixty-seven becomes a pay raise upon reaching FRA.

Second, not all retirement income is considered wage income.

For the purpose of the wage-related earnings limit, the SSA considers only the wages you earn while working for someone else as well as any income from self-employment. For the self-employed, only the net earnings from a business—as opposed to total revenue—is considered for the purpose of establishing wage earnings.

The SSA does not consider as wage earnings any income from other government benefits, or from investment dividends, pensions, common interest, annuity payments, or capital gains. However, an employee's contribution to a company's pension or retirement plan is considered part of wage earnings if the contribution is part of the employee's gross wages.

Third, let's note how the timing of wages earned affects the annual benefit.

For those working for wages, such wages count as part of your earnings limit in the year they are earned. For self-employed people, income counts against the earnings limit in the year it is received as opposed to when it was earned.

Fourth, the SSA has an interest in the amount of time a self-employed person spends in a retirement business prior to reaching FRA. This is, in short, one way for the SSA to determine whether a person taking early retirement benefits is really, truly retired. According to rules placed in in 2017, a person who works more than forty-five hours a month in self-employment is not considered to be truly retired.[11]

Fifth, any reduction in your benefit due to exceeding the annual earnings limit also affects any survivor or spousal benefit that is based upon your benefit. Note, though, wages earned by a spouse or eligible surviving children receiving benefits do not count against your annual earnings limit.

Finally, let's look at a special rule for wages earned in the first year of receiving "early" Social Security benefits.

People who "retire" and begin taking early benefits in the middle or later part of a calendar year often have exceeded the annual earnings limit before they stop working. Such people can still receive their full Social Security benefit, however, if their "post retirement" average monthly earnings for the rest of that first year do not exceed $1,470 a month (in 2019). Anything above that and the SSA considers you to be still employed and can reduce your monthly benefit.

---

[11] Social Security Administration. 2018. "How Work Affects Your Benefits." https://www.ssa.gov/pubs/EN-05-10069.pdf.

To work or not to work

For some people who elect to take Social Security early, the prospect of reduced benefits when exceeding the annual earnings limit is viewed as a penalty, a deterrent to working and earning as much as they would like in retirement.

Many of these people understand that money taken out now will eventually be returned after they reach FRA. Even so, some consciously choose to restrict their wage or self-employment earnings in order to retain every cent of a benefit that already has been reduced by their decision to begin taking benefits early.

It's a decision many people have to make upon taking "early retirement," and there is no set answer for everyone. As for myself, though, I've advised more people than not to earn the extra money when it is available, regardless of its immediate effect on Social Security benefits. The bird in hand usually looks better to me than the one in the bush.

I think back to a very real client, a woman who started taking benefits at age sixty-three, three years before her FRA at age sixty-six. Her son, a dentist with a small practice in need of a receptionist, said he needed help in the office on a part-time basis and asked if she would be interested in the job. She would be making around $25,000 a year and was very concerned about what this would do to her benefits and her tax situation. Would she be making a mistake, she asked, to take that kind of position?

To help address her question, we first broke down the mathematics of the situation.

She would be making about $10,000 over the allowed annual wage limit, which was around $15,000 at the time. On a more positive note, her son was able to add money to his group health plan, saving her about $6,000 a year in health insurance premiums. Still, the SSA would take back $5,000 in benefits—half of that $10,000, or $1 out for every $2 earned above the limit. She was receiving around $2,000 a month in benefits before taking the job. After taking the job, she will not receive a monthly check for three months until that $5,000 reduction is realized.

(A technical note here. My engineer clients will correctly note that the $5,000 reduction could have been achieved in only two-and-one-half months. But because Social Security is paid on a monthly basis, the SSA will withhold her regular $2,000 monthly benefit for three pay periods—a $6,000 total take back—then pay back the extra $1,000 it withheld in January of the following year.)

Remember here, any benefit withheld before FRA will be restored over time after reaching full retirement age. Remember also there is no limit on wage earnings after FRA.

If this woman should work three-plus years (at ages sixty-three, sixty-four, sixty-five, and part of sixty-six, the year she reaches FRA) at the same salary, she might have a total of around $15,000 in benefits withheld—possibly less, as the earnings limit increases each year. (Explanation: She was making roughly $10,000 a year more than the sliding earning limits at ages sixty-three, sixty-four, and sixty-five, or roughly $30,000 total of which the SSA will take back half. Remember, though, that she can receive up to $44,880 in the months of the year of her FRA, meaning that at age sixty-six she is under that limit with a $25,000 annual salary.)

Consequently, she will not receive her $2,000 monthly benefit for seven or eight months during that time. But, the income she is not getting from Social Security is more than being replaced by her employment income. Moreover, upon reaching FRA, she will receive what is essentially an immediate pay hike in monthly benefits as the withheld $15,000 is gradually repaid.

The bottom line, as I see it, is earning wages above the SSA allowable limit isn't a completely negative thing for people taking early benefits. For one thing, this woman will get those missing benefits back eventually. For another, she has the chance to help her son and herself, as she was bored silly and looking for something to do.

Keep in mind, however, what we said in the previous chapter about "torpedo taxes"—that is, how increases in income can affect the provisional income levels that determine how much of your Social Security will be taxed.

Remember the Social Security component of the provisional income formula is based on benefits received in a particular year. In the above example of the lady working for her dentist son after taking early benefits, her Social Security number in the provisional income formula would be her full $24,000 annual benefit in her first year of working—her regular $2,000 monthly benefit received for twelve months. In the second year, however, after she made $10,000 more than the earnings limit the previous year and the SSA takes back half ($5,000), her Social Security number in the provisional income formula is reduced to $19,000 ($24,000 minus the $5,000 take-back).

The prior example illustrates why your decision on when to begin taking benefits must be part of a comprehensive plan as opposed to simply asking, "How much benefit will I get when starting early compared to waiting until FRA or delaying till age seventy?"

Consider all factors that might come into play. Will you continue to work in some capacity? Will part-time wages compensate for a possible loss of benefits? Will part-time work leave you better able to pay health insurance premiums in the years before you become eligible for Medicare at age sixty-five? Can you afford to take less in Social Security benefits now knowing whatever you lose to earning limits will be returned to you over time after your reach FRA?

These are decisions that can't be made in a vacuum. This is often the place where a retirement planner with a full understanding of Social Security rules and their implications can be especially helpful to you.

Let's look at another situation in which incurring a "take back" for exceeding the wage limitation on people taking benefits before reaching FRA is not a completely bad thing.

Mary unexpectedly became a widow at age fifty-eight. She continued working to support herself, and at age sixty—the earliest age she could do so—she started taking a $1,500 monthly survivor benefit based on the earnings history of her late husband. That benefit wasn't enough to support her, so Mary kept working and consequently exceeded the earnings limit. The SSA, in turn, paid her survivor benefits for only four months over each of the next several years, but that $6,000 in annual income allowed her to visit out-of-town family, something she might not have been able to do without the benefit payment.

Mary continued to work until her full retirement age of sixty-six, at which time she got a "pay raise"—reimbursement for the "take backs" of the previous years. Moreover, at any time after FRA, Mary could switch from a survivor benefit to her personal work-history benefit that had grown over her years of continual employment. If she holds off taking her personal benefit until age seventy, she will receive an even bigger pay hike because of delayed retirement credits.

CHAPTER 7

Spousal Benefits
and Coordination

Had I written this book before the spring of 2016, you'd be reading here about some really cool options allowing for the maximization of Social Security benefits through spousal coordination strategies.

We would have been talking about some slick concepts such as "file and suspend." This was a strategy in which one spouse— typically the higher earner in a couple—would begin taking benefits, thus making the other spouse eligible for a spousal benefit equal to one-half of the higher earner's benefit. The higher earner would then voluntarily suspend taking benefits even as the lower-earning spouse continued taking a spousal benefit. The higher-earning spouse, in turn, would see his or her own benefit grow by 8 percent each a year (through delayed retirement credits earned after reaching FRA) until he or she resumed taking their now-enhanced benefit at age seventy.

Pretty neat concept, right? It sure was. It was so good, in fact, that the Social Security Administration got Congress to make it unavailable to anyone not already employing the strategy before

April 30, 2016, calling it an "unintended loophole" that was giving married couples benefits that were never intended.[12]

The SSA wasn't done in closing wide-open, beckoning loopholes. In the Bipartisan Budget Act of 2015, which took effect the following year, it also turned off the popular "restricted application" process for people who turned sixty-two on or after January 2, 2016.

Before this change was implemented, the restricted application allowed a person at full retirement age to apply for either a spousal benefit—provided their spouse was receiving benefits—or their own personal work-history benefit, whichever was greater. Any person taking a spousal benefit could see their own work-history benefit grow in value—again, 8 percent a year through delayed retirement credits—until they switched to their now enhanced work benefit at age seventy.

Yeah, that was another slick strategy, so good that the restricted application is no longer available to anyone born on or after January 2, 1954. (Important note: This rule change *does not* apply to survivor benefits for a widow or widower. More on that in our next chapter on survivor benefits.) However, note that even with the rule change, a small window remains open to people born before January 2, 1954 who have not yet filed for benefits. We'll talk briefly later in this chapter about options open to those few folks.

For now, let's concentrate on the spousal benefits that remain available to the majority of people reading this book who are probably still considering when to begin taking benefits and how to do so.

---

[12] Technically, Social Security benefits can still be suspended. You can stop taking benefits anytime you choose, but there are no ancillary benefits for a spouse or a child in doing so. A spouse or child cannot receive benefits while a worker's Social Security is suspended, thus making the "file and suspend" strategy null and void as it pertains to spousal coordination planning.

Spousal benefits at a glance

The concept of the spousal benefit was designed to extend the retirement safety net to spouses who had no or only a limited work history. The government, recognizing the importance of stay-at-home parenting where hard work is rarely rewarded by wages, set up a system whereupon a spouse at full retirement age (FRA) can receive a benefit of one-half of a spouse's benefit. To repeat a point mentioned earlier, in most cases, the lower-earning spouse takes a benefit based on that of the higher earner, but it doesn't have to work that way.

Several things to note quickly here.

A spousal benefit will never exceed more than one-half of the other spouse's benefit at the other spouse's full retirement age. In other words, even if the higher earner delays taking benefits until age seventy, thus allowing his own personal benefit to grow by 8 percent each year between FRA and the start of benefits, the spousal benefit created *does not* increase accordingly. Its level is frozen at half the value of the higher earner's PIA at the time of the higher earner's FRA.

On a similar note, a lower-earning spouse eligible for a spousal benefit who declines to take that benefit at FRA—perhaps because they are still working and the family doesn't need the extra income—is making a mistake in thinking that spousal benefit will grow in the years after FRA. No, it won't, and that's why it's a mistake to not take an available spousal benefit—if it works to your advantage; that is, if the spousal benefit is greater than your personal benefit—upon reaching your FRA.

We'll address this common misconception in our Chapter 9, "Common Mistakes, Special Situations," and show an example of how the spousal benefit is paid when the higher earner waits until age seventy to begin taking benefits.

Conversely, you will see your spousal benefit reduced in size if you begin taking it prior to reaching your own FRA. Just as is the case with your personal benefit being reduced when taken before FRA, so too is your spousal benefit reduced by the amount of time between when you started taking the "early" spousal benefit and your FRA.

> *Another myth about Social Security we need to debunk here is the notion that a spousal benefit is always one-half of the benefit— presumably the higher-earner's benefit—upon which it is based. Sometimes, that spousal benefit can actually be higher than half of the other spouse's benefit.*
>
> *Example: Al takes his personal benefit early and sees his project-ed $2,000 benefit at FRA reduced to $1,500. If his spouse, Peg, takes a spousal benefit before her FRA, <u>she will see a reduced $750 benefit</u>. But, if Peg waits until reaching her FRA to take her spousal benefit, she will receive the full $1,000 benefit based on what Al's benefit would have been at his FRA.*

Note, a person can begin taking spousal benefits as early as age sixty-two provided 1) their spouse has filed to receive benefits; and 2) they are either currently married or were in a marriage for ten years before being divorced.

That's right, divorced spouses can apply for spousal benefits based on the earnings of an ex, assuming the person seeking the benefit is not currently remarried. Some special rules apply, such as the ten-year previous marriage provision noted above. Also, not only must the divorced spouse seeking the benefit remain single, but they must have been divorced for a period of two years. (Again, the rules are different for a divorced *survivor* of a deceased ex. We will discuss those rules in the next chapter.)

On the positive side, a spousal benefit received by a former spouse does not affect the benefit of the ex, who doesn't even have to know that his or her former spouse is getting a benefit. The ex also need not have filed for one to begin receiving ex-spousal benefits—a situation completely opposite that of a married couple. The filing ex must be at least sixty-two to receive the benefit, however.

Spousal benefits after the 2016 changes

Sorry to be the bearer of bad news if you were counting on using the file-and-suspend or restricted application strategies you might have heard about previously. It's very likely you did, as both were very popular options recommended for years by many retirement advisors.

The file-and-suspend strategy was made ineffective as of April 30, 2016, and only families fortunate enough to have executed the strategy prior to that date can still do so effectively to coordinate spousal benefits. The filing of restricted applications, as noted above, has been discontinued for persons born on or after January 2, 1954.

Under the new rules in place today, most people eligible for both a spousal benefit and a personal benefit based on their own work history are deemed to have filed for both kinds of benefits upon making their first application. You will automatically receive the benefit that reflects the higher of the two amounts. You can no longer elect to take, for example, the lower spousal benefit while letting your personal work benefit grow until age seventy, at which time you switch to the enhanced personal benefit. (Once again, this discussion does not apply to survivor benefits.)

There is still an exception to this rule for people born prior to January 2, 1954. The restricted application process remains available to anyone whose date of birth beat the cutoff date and who has not yet filed for benefits.

Let's look at some examples of how things now work for two people of comparable, but slightly different ages.

Mary was born March 1, 1954, meaning she turned sixty-two after the January 2, 2016 restricted application cutoff date and had no opportunity to be "grandfathered" in. She worked most of her life as a homemaker, but also had some work history in the years before she started her family, then again after her grown kids left the nest. When she files for Social Security benefits at full retirement age (age sixty-six) in 2020, she will file an application that deems she is eligible for either a spousal benefit or a personal benefit from her own work history, whichever is greater. If Mary's husband has a $2,000 monthly benefit at his FRA, she would be eligible for a monthly spousal benefit of $1,000 when she reaches FRA. If her personal work history benefit was, say, $1,150, she would receive that higher amount each month.

But, let's say now that Mary was born December 30, 1953—just beating the cutoff date imposed by the Bipartisan Budget Act of 2015. She is effectively "grandfathered" under the former rules covering restricted applications.

Because she was lucky enough to have beaten the deadline by two days, upon reaching FRA in December of 2019, Mary can still file a restricted application by which she can choose to take either a spousal benefit or her own work history benefit—again, presuming her spouse is also taking a benefit that makes her eligible for spousal consideration. She might well elect to take the smaller spousal benefit ($1,000, using the same figures from the example above) and allow her work history benefit to grow by 8 percent a year over four years. At age seventy, she can switch over and now receive an enhanced personal benefit of some $1,518—a $368 monthly improvement over what she might have received at age 66 ($1,150).

In the real world, there probably aren't a lot of people for whom the restricted application is still an option. But, because there are some, and because it's a good opportunity to maximize your Social Security benefit, I wanted to mention it.

Frankly, I find too many retirement advisors don't raise this possibility in the aftermath of the 2015 changes. Too many seem to think the "good old days" when you could maximize Social Security benefits through file-and-suspend or restricted applications are over, and for many people they are.

At the same time, though, the restricted application window isn't closed for everyone, though it will be shortly. For those of you reading this book who were born before January 2, 1954 and have not made your decision on when and how to begin taking Social Security benefits, you may still have spousal coordination options available. You need to understand the importance of consulting with a financial advisor who works deep within the myriad complicated rules of Social Security, who understands what is available and what isn't. You need someone who keeps current about changing rules and newly developing strategies, and who might help you head off a long-term costly mistake that can't be fixed.

Many of the options of yesterday have disappeared, to be sure. But that doesn't mean you can afford not to plan ahead for tomorrow.

A situation I see occasionally involves a lower-earning spouse— let's call her Edith—who takes a reduced early personal benefit at a time before her higher-earning spouse (Archie) takes any benefit at all. Keep in mind, until Archie starts taking his benefits, Edith is not eligible for a spousal benefit. But, when Archie starts taking benefits (presumably at his FRA), Edith may well find that her now-available spousal benefit—half of what Archie gets if Edith waits until her FRA to claim it—is greater than her own reduced personal benefit.

The point here is to illustrate that, even with the end of the restricted application option for most people, there are still some spousal coordination opportunities available. This is where it is advisable to talk to someone knowledgeable about Social Security to discover options that might be available to you. Remember, the Social Security Administration—while able to answer any specific question you might have about such an opportunity—will not volunteer information about options that might work best in your particular situation.

CHAPTER **8**

Survivor Benefits

Despite all the concerns occasionally expressed about Social Security—most notably regarding its long-term viability, a concern I believe to be overstated—public opinion polls suggest the overwhelming majority of Americans believe the system does a lot of things right and is a program worth saving. [13]

I couldn't agree more. This is especially true when considering the safety net Social Security provides to widows, widowers, and surviving divorced spouses. It's in this area of survivor benefits that the program offers some of its most generous options.

Now, let's state the obvious at the start of this sometimes morbid discussion by noting the loss of a loved one is among the most difficult things any of us will face in life. No amount of Social Security benefit, insurance payment, or inheritance can completely salve that pain.

That's why it seems somewhat crass—although necessary—to point out that survivors often have it better than a lot of other Social Security beneficiaries. Please don't misunderstand me; the potential benefits that might be realized aren't worth the prospect of

[13] National Academy of Social Insurance. "Public opinions on Social Security." https://www.nasi.org/learn/social-security/public-opinions-social-security.

being locked up in prison. Even so, gallows humor occasionally seeps into client conversations about survivor benefits when even the most loving of spouses will jokingly ask what is being served for dinner tonight, and who will be cooking?

But enough of the funeral talk. Let's talk instead about the more positive aspects of survivor benefits, a form of federally provided life insurance that the Social Security Administration estimates is being used by some 5 million Americans today, many of them widows who are holding off poverty.

Survivor benefits at a glance

Let's go straight to the bottom line on survivor benefits. That is, upon the death of a spouse who has enough lifetime work credits (forty, or a ten-year work history) to qualify for Social Security benefits, a surviving widow or widower who is at least age sixty (with some exceptions we'll discuss shortly) becomes eligible to receive a survivor benefit as well as a $255 one-time lump sum payment. (Don't spend that one-time payment all in one place.)

The amount of that benefit depends on several factors, among them:

- The age of the survivor, and that of the deceased.
- The full retirement age (FRA) of both the survivor and the deceased.
- Whether the survivor or the deceased had started taking Social Security benefits, and when they began taking them.
- Whether the survivor has a disability, is caring for a child with a disability, or is caring for a minor child.

Clearly, there are multiple options here to examine. We'll do so by looking at examples illustrating each instance.

But let's begin with some basic rules, such as noting that survivor benefits—like all other aspects of Social Security—depend heavily on FRA.

A person eligible for a survivor benefit can receive a full benefit—that is, 100 percent of the benefit earned by the deceased at the time of death—by waiting until the survivor's FRA to claim it. Claiming a survivor benefit before FRA reduces its amount by anywhere from 28.5 percent to a mere 1 percent, depending on the amount of time between when a survivor begins taking a survivor benefit and the time of their FRA. The closer the survivor is to their FRA, the lower the reduction. Again, this reduction for survivors taking "early" benefits is based on theorizing, because you will receive more benefits payments over your remaining years, the size of each payment must be reduced.

Moreover, the FRA of the deceased is a factor in determining the amount of the survivor benefit, as is when or if the deceased began receiving benefits.

As we discussed earlier in the book, a worker who begins taking benefits before reaching FRA receives a reduced benefit. This in turn establishes a permanently reduced baseline for his survivor's benefit. But, a worker who waits until FRA to begin taking benefits receives a full benefit that also becomes available to a surviving spouse at their FRA. Better yet, a worker delaying benefits beyond FRA enhances that benefit—again, by 8 percent a year between FRA and age seventy—with a surviving spouse having that greater benefit available as a survivor option.

I don't know how many times I've visited with a married male client who will say, in essence, 'There's no history of longevity in my family; I don't think any male in my family has lived to see age seventy. So, I'm going to take what I can when I can from my Social Security, starting at age sixty-two.'

Then I talk with this gentleman's wife and she tells me, "Women in my family tend to live a long time. My mother is still alive at ninety, and her mother lived longer than that."

Well, we've got a problem here. Because the husband didn't think he would live long and wanted to get something out of the Social Security fund he'd been paying into for years, he starts his benefits at age sixty-two and establishes a reduced level of survivor benefit that his wife may be living on for another thirty years. That's a large pool of money left on the table over an extended period of time.

This is an example of what I've come to call "me vs. we" thinking. Simply put, sometimes people in a marriage fail to consider what is best in the long term for a surviving partner as opposed to their individual interest. The husband, in this case, did not know that even if he passed before taking benefits at FRA, his widow would be eligible for a survivor benefit based on the considerably greater benefit he would have received had he been alive to see FRA.

Again, such a decision is a highly individualized one, and there is no one solution for every situation. Still, I generally encourage people to think in terms of "we" as opposed to "me" when making their critical long-term Social Security decisions.

We talk about "options" here because a widow or widower might have some interesting choices, a chance to maximize lifetime Social Security benefits depending on whether or not the survivor has begun taking benefits. These are, we should add, survivor benefit options that are no longer available for spousal benefits following the 2015 legislative action described in Chapter 7.

One additional note here. If you are receiving a spousal benefit, which is usually up to one-half of your spouse's benefit (as detailed in Chapter 7), you can switch to a more lucrative survivor benefit when your spouse dies. The survivor benefit, remember, can be as much as 100 percent of the deceased's benefit if the proper conditions are met.

The best-case scenario at the worst possible time

Even at this horrible time in a person's life following the death of a long-time mate, a surviving spouse who has not yet begun taking benefits faces some interesting options with the potential for long-term financial impact.

A survivor in this situation can choose, beginning at age sixty, to take either a survivor's benefit or their own personal work-history benefit. This decision is not set in stone, however, as most other Social Security decisions are. Such a person might, for instance, take a survivor benefit for a number of years while letting their personal benefit grow until it maxes out at age seventy. At that time, the survivor has the option to switch over to their personal benefit should it now exceed the survivor benefit.

Example: Bill passes away at age sixty-eight, just two years after he started taking benefits at his FRA of sixty-six. His monthly benefit was $2,200 at the time of his death. His younger wife, Mary, sixty-four, had planned to wait two years until her FRA (also sixty-six) before starting to take her work-history benefits that were projected to be $1,800 monthly.

Following Bill's death, however, Mary suddenly needs income and she begins taking Bill's survivor benefit. By taking that survivor benefit at age sixty-four, two years before her FRA, her survivor benefit will be reduced by about 9.5 percent. Had Mary waited two years until her FRA, she could have received 100 percent of Bill's benefit, the full $2,200.

But Mary's decision here is not final. For, even as she is taking the survivor benefit, her personal work-history account continues to grow through delayed retirement credits until at age seventy it has increased by some 32 percent over its FRA value (projected to be $1,800) to a $2,376 monthly benefit. Mary at this point can switch from the survivor benefit to her more lucrative personal benefit and receive a higher monthly payment for the rest of her years.

A more common scenario; both spouses collecting benefits

More typical is a case where both members of a couple are receiving benefits—typical given the average life expectancy of seventy-six for American men and eighty-one for U.S. women.[14] In this much-more-common scenario, the surviving spouse's benefit becomes the greater of the two benefits the couple received while both were alive. The lesser of the two benefits disappears completely. There are no choices to be made.

In a typical case where both married spouses are taking Social Security benefits, the key element in the planning process happens when they first decide to take benefits. I've talked throughout this book about the wisdom of waiting until FRA or beyond to take benefits. Not everyone chooses to do that for a variety of reasons, but that decision can have consequences for both the living and the dead.

Let's consider this true case involving a prospective client:

This man was several months past his sixty-second birthday when I first met him. Tragically, he had terminal pancreatic cancer and said he knew he wouldn't live to see his FRA at age sixty-six. He consequently started taking Social Security benefits at sixty-two, his earliest possible age. His wife, a very healthy tennis player, had never worked outside the house and had basically nothing in work-history credits toward her own benefit.

I understand, I truly do, why this man wanted to get something while he was living—anything—from the Social Security pool into

[14] Statistica. 2018. "Average Life Expectancy in North America for Those Born in 2018, by Gender and Region (in Years)."

https://www.statista.com/statistics/274513/life-expectancy-in-north-america/

which he'd been paying for years. Unfortunately, in doing so, he reduced his benefit by 25 percent, which in turn permanently reduced his wife's survivor benefit by 25 percent for the rest of her life.

Had I met him before he made his decision, I could have laid out some facts he did not know. I would have told him that if he *did not* take benefits at age sixty-two, his surviving wife at the time of his death would have received a survivor benefit based on what he *would have received* at age sixty-six, his FRA. Had he made an admittedly difficult decision to not take benefits during whatever time he had remaining, he might well have increased his wife's lifetime benefit following his death by 25 percent.

Conversely, a person who delays taking benefits until after FRA makes an enhanced benefit available to a surviving spouse. For example: The surviving spouse of a worker who dies at age sixty-eight without ever filing for benefits is eligible for a survivor benefit based on what the deceased would have received at the time of death.

Note, however, that this enhanced benefit will never be greater than it is at age seventy. A common mistake I see far too often is a spouse who delays taking benefits beyond age seventy in the mistaken belief that he or she is increasing a spouse's benefit. That isn't happening, which is why I advise against delaying the start of benefits beyond age seventy.

This brings us back to the concept I touched on earlier in this chapter, one I call "we versus me." Translated, it means thinking long-term of your prospective surviving spouse when making your choice on when to take benefits. At the same time, you must realize that you can only do so much for a spouse, and that the opportunities to boost a potential Social Security benefit pretty much end at age seventy.

We talked briefly in Chapter 3 about how it is possible to reset your initial decision on taking Social Security benefits if the change is made in the first twelve months and you pay back the benefits you received.

A real story here illustrates how this can sometimes be a good option, even if in the most horrible of circumstances.

This man knew he had cancer when he started taking his Social Security benefits early at age sixty-three, but he learned he was terminal within the next year. In his case, we advised him to visit with a Social Security attorney and explore the possibility of filing for disability. This would mitigate the reduction of benefits he incurred when filing early, as well as give him additional income for himself and his family, and allow him to leave a larger death benefit to his survivors.

Had he not done this, his widow would have been left with the reduced benefit he received when he started taking benefits early. By resetting his option, she became eligible for the full benefit to which he was entitled had he lived to his FRA. It turned out to be worth several thousand extra dollars a year for her.

Here is a case where I strongly suspect the average advisor might have told this man to take the benefits early, as his family likely needed the income to deal with medical bills. But an advisor well versed in Social Security rules would have seen this other disability option that might ultimately prove more beneficial to the widow years down the road.

I can't emphasize enough the importance of having your advisor coordinate efforts with legal professionals when you find yourself in a complicated situation such as disability and end-of-life planning.

Divorced spouses

Survivor benefits also can be paid to a divorced surviving spouse age sixty or older. To qualify, the survivor must have been married to the deceased for at least ten years and did not remarry before age sixty.

Exceptions: A disabled divorced spouse can begin receiving survivor benefits at age fifty. Also, a divorced survivor who has not remarried and who is caring for a minor child of the deceased, or a disabled child, can receive a benefit at any age.

If a divorced surviving spouse is caring for a minor or disabled child of the deceased, they **need not** have been married to the deceased for ten years. See the following section for more details.

Let's also note here that a divorced person who remarries after age sixty not only can receive a survivor benefit from a deceased ex, but also can claim a spousal benefit from their current mate beginning at age sixty-two. As noted at the beginning of the chapter, Social Security has a soft spot for widows and widowers.

Younger/disabled survivors, children and dependent parents

As noted above, survivor benefits can be taken as early as age fifty if the survivor is disabled and the disability began before or within seven years of the deceased worker's death. A survivor benefit also can be taken at any age by a widow or widower who has not remarried and is caring for a deceased worker's minor child under the age of sixteen, or is caring for a disabled child who is receiving benefits based on the earnings record of the deceased. The child must be the natural or legally adopted child of the surviving spouse and the deceased.

Unmarried children under the age of eighteen, or age nineteen if still attending elementary or secondary school full time, also are eligible for survivor benefits from a qualified deceased worker. In 2017, the Social Security Administration reported ninety-eight out of every one hundred0 children meeting the above qualification could receive benefits, should a working parent die.[15] Also, a child who became disabled before age twenty-two and who remains disabled is eligible for benefits at any age.

Even the surviving dependent parents of a deceased worker can be eligible for a survivor benefit provided they are age sixty-two or older and that the deceased provided for at least half of their support before passing.

The above-described benefits depend, as do all Social Security benefits, upon how much the deceased put into the system before passing. The deceased worker's basic benefit establishes a baseline upon which the survivor benefit is based.

A widow or widower of any age caring for a child under sixteen is eligible to receive 75 percent of the deceased worker's benefit amount. A child eligible to receive a benefit also can receive 75 percent of that benefit.

Note here there is a family limit on benefits received. This limit might apply if a widow with surviving children were receiving benefits from the work record of a deceased spouse/parent. The limit varies between 150 and 180 percent of the deceased's base benefit.[16]

How to apply for a survivor benefit

It can't be done online as you can do for a regular benefit. It has to be done through direct contact with the Social Security Administration, either via phone (800-772-1213) or by visiting a regional SSA office. (Hint: Setting up an appointment in advance might save you time when visiting the office.)

---

[15] Social Security Administration. "Survivor Benefits." 2018.
https://www.ssa.gov/pubs/EN-05-10084.pdf.
[16] Ibid.

The SSA advises a surviving spouse to make this contact reasonably soon after dealing with the other difficult matters following a mate's death. Many benefit payments, the SSA notes, are based on the time you apply as opposed to the date of your loved one's death.

Be prepared to bring along some essential information, such as:

- Proof of death, either via a state-issued death certificate or one from a funeral home.
- Social Security numbers of both yourself and the deceased.
- Your birth certificate.
- Your marriage certificate, if a widow or widower.
- Divorce papers, if applying as a divorced spouse.
- The deceased worker's W-2 form or federal self-employment tax form from the previous year.
- Birth certificates and Social Security numbers, if available, for any minor children who will be applying for benefits.

A lot of forms, to be sure, but the SSA sometimes can be helpful in securing official documents you might not be able to access.

Note, too, there are several things a thoughtful spouse can do while living to prepare his loved ones for the time when he isn't. Even if retirement is years away, but especially as it draws near, reviewing your personal Social Security information at socialsecurity.gov/myaccount can be very helpful.

Once you register (a relatively painless process) and log-in, you can access an estimate of your benefit based on your current age and work history coupled with different ages at which you might retire. You can also find information regarding potential survivor benefits. You can also request a replacement Social Security card or Medicare card, as well as obtain other helpful information.

The bottom line

Good retirement planning takes into account two scenarios. First, can retirement assets be stretched out long enough to cover a couple should both spouses live to age 120? No, that isn't likely to happen but, by planning for an unlikely extreme, you should feel good about having all the more realistic bases covered.

Second, and the more likely occurrence: Will a surviving spouse be able to continue a comparable lifestyle following the death of a mate, especially one who was the higher earner of the two?

A well-designed Social Security strategy can go a long way toward meeting both extremes. Planning to maximize a survivor's benefit is a critical component of such a strategy. For, while we can anticipate future changes coming in Social Security options—changes that seem inevitable with some 10,000 baby boomers retiring on a nearly daily basis these days—we have reason to believe many of the survivor benefits discussed in this chapter are something of a sacred cow. That is, they are options in place today that are likely to remain in place for years to come.

CHAPTER 9

Common Mistakes, Special Situations

L et's take a capsule look at what I consider some common mistakes I see clients making frequently, noted here not to belittle them but to help you avoid situations that could have potential pitfalls.

Common mistakes

Example One

Two people in a married couple are both over the age of seventy, yet neither is taking benefits because one or both are still working, or they have considerable other retirement income and simply don't need the additional Social Security income.

Simply put, waiting past age seventy to begin taking benefits is always a mistake. There is never, ever a reason—even if you are still working or have significant other retirement assets—to wait beyond age seventy to begin taking benefits. There is simply nothing to be gained by waiting. The delayed retirement credits that enhance a benefit by 8 percent a year when those benefits are not taken at full retirement age end at age seventy, meaning your benefit will never be higher (except for minor cost-of-living adjustments) than it is then.

Beyond that, you're leaving money on the table. Someone is offering you a paycheck—money you have coming to you—that you're not taking. It's just plain silly. There is no situation I can see that would prevent a person from taking benefits at age seventy.

Put it another way. You're walking out your door when you see a check for $3,000 payable to you lying on the floor. Would you leave that check where you found it? Didn't think so.

Okay, so maybe you're fine financially without the additional Social Security income. Congratulations if this is the case. Still, you can always invest any Social Security benefit you don't absolutely need as income and grow it for a later time when you might need it for a health emergency, or for long-term nursing care, or to leave as a legacy for heirs, or maybe for charitable giving. Maybe you can do a bit of all of the above.

An option for consideration. You might want to think about converting a Social Security benefit you don't need into an investment that can be passed on tax free to heirs, or maybe explore charitable endeavors. Leveraging unneeded RMDs or Social Security benefits into the purchase of life insurance, with its tax-free death benefit for beneficiaries, is sometimes an option for people who can still get insurance at this age.

Example Two

Wilma, who did only limited work outside the home, is eligible for a benefit based on spouse Fred's more extensive work history. This spousal benefit is considerably more than Wilma's own limited work-history benefit. Yet, Wilma doesn't take the benefit at age sixty-six or sixty-seven, thinking it will grow if she waits until age seventy to begin taking benefits.

Sorry, Wilma, but it won't. Wilma's spousal benefit will never be greater than it is at Fred's full retirement age. True, Fred's personal work-history benefit will grow through delayed retirement credits if he waits to age seventy to take it, but any spousal benefit for Wilma is frozen at Fred's FRA.

Illustration: Fred's monthly benefit at FRA was $2,200, meaning Wilma's spousal benefit at her FRA was $1,100. Fred's personal benefit might grow to $2,900 by waiting until age seventy to take benefits, but Wilma won't receive $1,450 at that point. Her $1,100 benefit is fixed at Fred's FRA.

Example Three

Widows and widowers who are eligible for a survivor benefit at age sixty but are not collecting.

They really need to start doing so, or at least looking into it. Remember, widows and widowers have available options—i.e., the ability to choose between a survivor benefit or their own personal work-history benefit, depending on which is greater—that are not available to everyone else after the changes of 2015. They still have the chance to take a survivor benefit, then switch to their enhanced personal benefit at a later time if it is more beneficial.

Moreover, if you are a surviving spouse with minor children (under age sixteen) in your home, you should take a survivor benefit (if available from the deceased spouse) regardless of age. Keep in mind this benefit may be reduced by the survivor's working status and age, but it is still a benefit that can be most helpful in dealing with the loss of a spouse and the household income that spouse was providing to a young family.

It is often helpful in this case to consult with a professional—either with an SSA representative or someone with an extensive knowledge of Social Security rules—to find out exactly what is available both to you as a surviving spouse as well as to the surviving minor children of the deceased. Social Security's rules for widows and surviving minor children have a considerable bit of leniency, but in rare situations there can be adverse consequences if benefits are not taken correctly. So, again, it's best to visit with a professional who can guide you through the process.

Example Four

A person with a full work history who continues to work beyond the time they would like to retire on the belief that they can grow their Primary Insurance Amount (PIA) and increase their Social Security benefit.

The methods and formulas used by the Social Security Administration to determine a worker's PIA are complicated, and if you really want to get into the weeds you can find the details at the SSA website (ssa.gov).[17]

The bottom line, however, is that a person with a full work history will generally help themselves minimally by working longer than they would like to. This is because a worker's PIA is an average of the thirty-five highest earning years of that worker's career, and that thirty-five-year average isn't going to grow appreciably with some extra couple years of work. Even if you are in your peak earning years at the end of your career (as most people are), an extra year or two of work might increase your benefit only minimally—probably not enough to make a difference on choosing whether to retire or not.

There are, however, a couple groups of people for whom working longer later in life can be very beneficial and ought to be considered.

One group is federal government workers who paid a percentage of their salary into the Civil Service Retirement System (CSRS) as opposed to the Social Security system. (Note: People who began working for the federal government after January 1, 1987, are part of the Federal Employees Retirement System, or

---

[17] Social Security Administration. 2018. "Social Security Benefits Amounts."
https://www.ssa.gov/oact/cola/Benefits.html

FERS, which features payments to and benefits from Social Security.)[18] People who paid exclusively into CSRS may not have a significant PIA for Social Security, and they might want to increase that pool in order to complement pension payments they receive from CSRS based on their years in that system.

Illustration: Let's look at someone who worked twenty years for the federal government and paid into CSRS for that entire period. This person then left federal employment and began a twenty-year career in private industry. Now, at age sixty, this person who has worked for forty years finds themselves with only a twenty-year PIA with Social Security. They want to increase that number in order to receive a larger Social Security benefit to complement whatever they receive in pension payments from CSRS. Such a person could help themselves considerably by working several years beyond their hoped-for retirement age. Should such a person work up to an additional ten years before taking SS benefits at age seventy, they've effectively grown their PIA number as well as enhanced their ultimate benefit through delayed retirement credits.

Another group that could help itself with extra years of work are people who went unemployed for several years and consequently have low numbers (or zeros) for those years on their thirty-five-year "box score" of highest earnings. For people in such a situation—one becoming ever-more-commonplace in today's era of job insecurity in many industries—the opportunity to work longer at a later point in life is a chance to plug some better numbers into their PIA formula and increase their Social Security benefit.

---

[18] Social Security Administration. 2018. "Retirement Planner: Federal Government Employment."
https://www.ssa.gov/planners/retire/fedgovees.html.

At the extreme end of this group are people, usually self-employed ones, who worked on a cash basis or did not otherwise fully report income or pay FICA taxes. Such folks often find themselves not only with a limited PIA, but occasionally without the forty work credits—typically amassed over a ten-year work history—required to receive not only Social Security but also basic Medicare coverage beginning at age sixty-five. For people in this kind of situation, working past a time when they would like to stop makes a lot of sense.

But again, I strongly suspect that the overwhelming majority of people with the foresight to be reading this book have a thirty-five-year history of earnings. An extra year or two of earnings isn't going to make a substantial difference for them.

Example Five

Assuming all financial advisors can answer every question regarding the transformation from the investment-based accumulation phase of life (i.e., our working years) into the income-based distribution phase (also known as retirement). Or, in a similar vein, assuming all advisors are fully prepared to help you find the best way to take your Social Security benefits.

Not all advisors are created equal. Don't just assume a broker, agent, or an insurance salesman—even one who has been helpful in building your portfolio in the past—is capable of addressing the matters described above, much less fully understanding all the myriad, complex nuances of Social Security.

How does a client know whether an advisor is prepared to handle distribution phase matters? Well, I would suggest, if you're dealing with someone more interested in selling you financial products, you're likely dealing with a transactional advisor instead of a transformational one. Let's be candid here: Commissions are made on the financial tools a broker, agent, or advisor sells. But there is no commission to be gained through helping people with Social Security and, consequently, a lot of brokers don't get deep into the weeds regarding one of the biggest components of many financial nest eggs.

Yes, tools are important. You don't build a house without a hammer, for instance. But you also don't wander through the local home building supply store tossing tools and supplies into your shopping cart without first having a specific plan. That plan dictates what tools and supplies you will need. Retirement planning is no different.

Special circumstances need special assistance

Although about 90 percent of Americans with enough work history will qualify to receive Social Security benefits, there are some people—even some with an extended work history—who will not.

An estimated 10 percent of Americans either do not have enough work history to qualify, or bypassed Social Security by paying instead into state or local government-approved pension programs. Examples of this latter group include civil service workers—police officers, firefighters, city utility workers—as well as some teacher's groups and clergy members. Much of their retirement income will flow from pension payments made by local or state government retirement programs into which they made withholding payments.

Many workers in the above groups, however, also have a work history that includes payments into the Social Security system, thus making them eligible for Social Security benefits in addition to the pension they receive from their civil service work. We're talking here, for example, about police officers who earn extra income working off-duty as bouncers or special event security, or teachers who work as painters or handymen during their summers vacations, etc.

Many of these people may find their Social Security benefit reduced, however, by the Windfall Elimination Provision (WEP). This provision effectively reduces a Social Security benefit by the amount of pension (or disability) paid by an employer—such as a government agency—who did not withhold Social Security taxes from your paycheck.[19]

A Social Security spousal or survivor benefit may also be reduced by the Government Pension Offset (GPO), a law that reduces a benefit paid to a spouse or survivor if the worker on whom the benefit is based receives a retirement or disability pension from a federal, state, or local government agency that did not pay Social Security payroll taxes.[20]

An exception to the reduced benefit provision is any federal, state, or local government employee whose government pension is from a job in which the worker paid Social Security taxes. Government workers under the Federal Employees Retirement System (FERS, described in Example 4 above), or government workers who switched from the Civil Service Retirement System into FERS, also are exempt from the possible benefit reduction.

The rules governing these plans, as well as the WEP and the GPO, can be complicated. Moreover, these local plans are vanishing, and only professionals with years of expertise with such plans may have enough knowledge of them to be able to give you the advice you need should you be covered by one. So, if you have not paid FICA withholding and think a special pension situation may apply to you, you need to visit with a professional who has exper-

---

[19] Social Security Administration. 2018. "Windfall Elimination Provision." https://www.ssa.gov/pubs/EN-05-10045.pdf.

[20] Social Security Administration. 2018. "Government Pension Offset." https://www.ssa.gov/pubs/EN-05-10007.pdf.

tise in the nuances of Social Security and can tell you how your special pension might affect your Social Security benefit.

I've been workin' on the railroad, lucky me

People who worked in the railroad industry sometimes have some exciting options available to them that deserve special attention.

This is because many American railroads maintained their own pension system, overseen by the Railroad Retirement Board, which went through several mutations that eventually included merging with the Social Security Administration in the 1980s. Consequently, many railroad workers have railroad benefit options in addition to those offered through Social Security.

Such options are too numerous to list in this book. But let's talk about just one of them, the opportunity to take an early retirement at a reduced benefit through the railroad retirement plan, then having an opportunity later to reset that benefit through Social Security at FRA. In effect, some railroad workers can receive a full Social Security benefit despite exercising the option to retire early under the old railroad plan. It's really a neat deal in that they are not penalized like the rest of us are when we take a benefit early.

The other thing I like about helping the occasional railroad worker I see is that it is easier getting help from the Railroad Retirement Board than it is from the Social Security Administration, in my opinion. If you are a railroad employee with pension questions, I highly recommend calling these people who do a good job of looking after their own.

Veterans, thank you for the service

If you served in the military, you've lived on domestic bases, ships or submarines at sea, or on military installations overseas—some of them in active war zones. Your fine-dining experiences included MREs and fast grabs from base commissaries. You may have been deployed to remote corners of the world, often at great danger to yourself. You lived a lifestyle those without military service cannot imagine.

Thank you for your service. I myself am a Marine Corps veteran. Many of my clients are also former U.S. military personnel, and what they and others need to know is their military service affects future Social Security benefits. It depends on when you served, so let's break it down and take a look.

Vietnam Era, 1957-1977

A historical note. Veterans who served in World War II and the Korean War did not pay into FICA during their service years. Military pay was not subject to FICA tax until January 1, 1957. Prior to then, the Social Security Administration credited a veteran's earnings record with a $160 wage credit for each month of active duty. These veterans, obviously, began receiving Social Security long before I even dreamed of writing this book.

For veterans who began service beginning in 1957 and after—a period that includes veterans of the Vietnam War such as my father—their military pay was subject to FICA taxes and became part of their earnings record. In addition, their earnings history was credited with a $300 credit for each quarter of active duty. (Those individual credits did not apply, however, to veterans who received a military pension.)

1978 through 2001

Veterans who served after 1978 continued to pay FICA tax on their military earnings. Social Security also credited them with an additional $100 for every $300 in active-duty basic pay received. This benefit had a maximum of $1200 annually. (Exception: Veterans enlisting after September 7, 1980 who did not complete twenty-four months of active duty might not be eligible for the additional $100 credit.)

2002 to present

In January 2002, the Defense Appropriations Act stopped the special extra earnings that had been credited to military service personnel. Military service in the calendar year 2002 and future years no longer qualifies for special extra earnings credits.[21]

However, veterans' benefits also have a provision through which a recipient receives a yearly increase in benefits beyond any cost-of-living adjustment made by the SSA. I haven't heard of any situations where a veteran did not receive this increase, but it's something veterans need to be aware of and to continually check to make sure they are receiving the automatic increase to which they are entitled.

Military pensions and Social Security

Service members who receive a military pension can also receive a Social Security benefit. However, there are numerous factors that can affect an individual's monthly payments. For example, if you receive a military disability pension and apply for Social Security, your total compensation becomes limited. Social Security payments also affect Veterans Administration pension payments.

---

[21] Social Security Administration. 2018. "Special Extra Earnings for Military Service." http://www.socialsecurity.gov/planners/retire/military.html.

Here again is another area where veterans need to be aware of additional Social Security benefits that might be available to them, but sometimes are overlooked. Veterans with questions about Social Security are well advised to consult someone with special knowledge about the relationship between Social Security and military pensions.

CHAPTER 10

Fitting the Puzzle Pieces Together, Seeing the Big Picture

I'm going to take a not-so-crazy guess here and venture that most readers of this book have worked on a puzzle at various points in their lives.

Maybe you did them as a child, probably with the assistance and encouragement of a parent or grandparent who may or may not have known they were helping you develop memory skills, spatial and pattern recognition, logical thinking, and problem-solving skills. Or, most likely, they turned you on to puzzles simply because they are fun and they enjoyed spending time with you.

Later in life, especially in our retirement years, puzzle solving is encouraged as a way of maintaining cognitive skills that diminish as we get older. Beyond that, many older people think puzzle solving is as much fun now as it was when they were kids.

So, for anyone who has ever worked a puzzle, let me ask a question: What are the most important parts of a puzzle?

Many people will point to the edge pieces that form the frame. Others say they work from the inside out. There is no one correct answer, obviously.

But let me provide an alternative reply for your consideration. That is, I believe the most important part of any puzzle is the picture on the box it came in.

It's the box cover, after all, that gives us the big picture of where we ultimately want to be in merging hundreds of pieces together. And that, in my roundabout way, brings us back to Social Security and its permanent effect on our overall retirement picture.

Retirement planning, I suspect you know by now, is a process of putting together numerous pieces of a financial puzzle. To solve that puzzle, however, you first need to see the overall picture of where you want to be before you start. That picture is one you have to envision for yourself. As a financial advisor, I simply **must** know where you realistically imagine yourself going in retirement before I can offer options on helping you get there.

Assembling the pieces is only the start

You know, I often see clients who have ten, twenty, even thirty pieces of a retirement puzzle spread across the table. They have investments in different brokerage accounts, IRAs in several places, a 401(k) here or a 403(b) there, several different annuities, maybe two or three life insurance policies, rental properties, maybe an inheritance and, of course, Social Security. Not surprisingly, many of them have no idea of how to fit all those pieces together.

Other clients have the opposite problem. They may have only two or three puzzle pieces, one of them being Social Security. They might have a big-view image of where they want to be, but they suspect they don't have enough pieces to get there.

The challenge in retirement planning, quite simply, is finding a way to fit together all the different financial puzzle pieces you've amassed over the accumulation years of your life. Or, to get the maximum value from the few pieces you might have while at the same time looking for new sources of income that may be available to you.

This book has been primarily about Social Security, which is just one piece of the retirement puzzle—albeit a very important one for many Americans. And while I've worked hard over my career to make myself as knowledgeable as I could about the complexities of Social Security, I'll be the first to admit it takes far more than extensive familiarity with Social Security to draw up a comprehensive retirement plan. Doing so requires an advisor with a background in harvesting income from different types of retirement accounts (qualified and non-qualified), dealing with tax issues that can be new in retirement, inheritance and legacy planning, providing spousal support, establishing funds for long-term care, and other issues.

Clearly, this requires more than a broker/agent who only sells products, however good those products might be as vehicles for retirement preparation.

This is why I respectfully suggest, as noted earlier in the book, that if you are working with an advisor who does not talk about the effect of taxes and inflation in retirement; one who does not discuss ways of maximizing Social Security through delaying benefits or using spousal coordination or limiting taxes on benefits; one who does not talk about moving tax-deferred retirement funds into tax-advantageous buckets such as Roth IRAs; one who does not forewarn of the "torpedo taxes" that come with RMDs; one who does not look ahead to the need for financing long-term care—then you are not dealing with a comprehensive retirement planner.

Just as we needed help as children upon first seeing a puzzle, so too do most of us need help in seeing the big puzzle that is our retirement.

I've talked in this book—and it bears repeating here—about people who for good reasons do the wrong things because they fail to see this big picture. The client, for instance, who tries to help his family's immediate budget needs by taking Social Security benefits at the earliest possible age, overlooking that, in doing so, he is permanently reducing a potential survivor benefit for his wife who, statistically, is likely to outlive him—possibly by many years.

This is why I say it's not enough in real retirement planning to merely make good investments. Once again, it's not what you earned that counts most in retirement. What counts most is how much you get to keep from what you've earned. To do that successfully takes real planning, a true understanding of how all the puzzle pieces fit together.

CHAPTER 11

The Value in Seeking Help

I began this book talking about how I set out to learn as much as I could about Social Security in an effort to help my dad, a smart man who felt he had nowhere to turn for answers to complex issues. In learning all I could to help him, I believe I developed a niche that could in turn help others.

Please allow me to close this book with one more personal story that illustrates a point.

My son was a premature arrival, weighing a mere three pounds and fifteen ounces at his birth two months before his projected due date. Good news first: I'm delighted to report ten years later he's playing hockey three times a week and is an accomplished math student. But in those first stressful days of his life, I saw first-hand the wonderful work done by specialists in neo-natal care, physicians and nurses who deal with people during the very short but tenuous first months of life.

It's what I work to do today in focusing on families in a relatively short but critical period of their life—the time when you have to make critical decisions about retirement. More precisely, it's the time when you have to make Social Security decisions that will stay with you for the rest of your life. It is critical to get those decisions right, which is why working with a retirement planner knowledgeable about Social Security is very important.

I say that based on the experience gained from working with hundreds of clients seeking to get the most from their Social Security benefits in particular, and from their overall retirement nest egg in general.

I wish I could say that more financial advisors took the time needed to familiarize themselves with the myriad complicated aspects of Social Security. Sadly, I can't do that.

Much of the reason for that has to do with the transactional nature of the financial services business. I believe the reason big brokerage firms spend so little time discussing Social Security in personal meetings or on their websites is there are no sales for them to make, no commissions to earn from dealing with Social Security.

Remember, too, that the Social Security Administration, while willing to answer your general questions, isn't allowed to offer specific advice on options. Nor will its representatives address issues that may not have occurred to you.

So, if your retirement planning includes specific concerns about the impact of Social Security, you need to seek the help of someone with specialized knowledge. Not every advisor has it.

An example: You can go into any typical small town and ask a local attorney, "Do you do business law?" Sure, he'll say, of course he's done some. "Do you do estate planning?" Of course, many attorneys do a little of everything, just as advisors in my industry do. But, are they really specialists in business law, estate planning or—in my industry—Social Security? These are questions worth asking when you are seeking help with a specific issue.

Again, don't misunderstand me here. There is a time and place in our working years when you can be perfectly comfortable with a broker or advisor who can guide you toward more aggressive investments designed for long-term growth and wealth accumulation.

As you approach and enter retirement, however, your needs change as you transition from the accumulation to distribution phase of life. Investments necessary to outpace inflation and re-place part of what we take as retirement income need to become more conservative in nature. That very capable agent who sold you successful investment products earlier in your life may not be as skilled in harvesting income later in life.

This is why I suggest that people nearing or entering retire-ment often need to seek the additional advice of Registered In-vestment Advisors, preferably someone who is also a CERTIFIED FINANCIAL PLANNER™ professional such as myself, someone who works extensively on retirement issues such as turning in-vestment assets into retirement income, who deals regularly with legacy planning, long-term care and Social Security.

May I also respectfully suggest that myself and my staff at Min-neapolis-based Secured Retirement Financial stand ready to help you with those issues.

Feel free to contact our office at 952-460-3260 or email my team at AskACFP@SecuredRetirments.com if you would like to contact us regarding a consultation on your specific Social Security questions.

Glossary

Although I've done my best to define all the special terms and jargon we use to talk about Social Security throughout this book, I thought it might also be helpful to revisit a few of the most often-used terms in this special glossary. Feel free to refer back to it while reading or when browsing through your Social Security benefit filing options.

AGI—shorthand for adjusted gross income, the total of your income, minus any exemptions or deductions, which the federal government uses to determine your tax rate.

COLA—shorthand for cost-of-living adjustments, which are annual adjustments to the monthly amount of Social Security benefits you receive, by law they are based on the Bureau of Labor Statistics' annual calculation of the national inflation rate.

Delayed Retirement Credits—an increase in your benefit by about 8 percent per year for every year you wait to begin receiving your benefits after your full retirement age.

Divorced Spouse Benefit—similar to a spousal benefit, you may qualify to take a divorced spouse benefit, up to 50 percent of your ex-spouse's benefit, if you were married for ten years (or are raising your ex-spouse's and your minor or disabled children) and have been divorced for at least two years, you are sixty-two, and you are unmarried. Your ex's marital status doesn't determine your ability to qualify, and, unlike spousal benefits, your ex-spouse needn't have filed for you to begin your benefits, nor do they receive a notice that you are taking benefits based on their earnings history.

FRA—shorthand for full retirement age, this is the age (based on your birthyear and month) at which the Social Security Administration deems you "ripe" to receive your full retirement benefit.

MAGI—shorthand for modified adjusted gross income, which is your regularly taxed adjusted gross income, plus any tax-exempt income you have, plus half your Social Security benefit, the total of which the federal government then uses to determine the rate at which to tax your Social Security benefits.

Provisional Income Formula—The formula by which the federal government calculates your modified-adjusted gross income, or what portion of your Social Security benefit may be subject to taxation; ½ Social Security + AGI + tax-exempt income.

RMD—abbreviation for required minimum distribution, the percentage of your IRA or 401(k) account you are federally required to withdraw every year after age seventy-and-one-half based off of your projected life expectancy; failure to withdraw your RMD in a given year could result in a 50 percent tax of your unwithdrawn RMD for that year.

Spousal Benefit—a benefit equal to as much as half of your spouse's benefit at full retirement age, which you might file to receive if you have a low or incomplete personal earnings history.

Survivor's Benefit—when one spouse dies, the surviving spouse will continue to receive the higher of the two's Social Security monthly checks, called a survivor's benefit.

SSA—shorthand for the Social Security Administration, the wing of the federal government that oversees the nation's Social Security benefits.

Acknowledgments

This book would never have been possible were it not for my parents, Joe and Barb Lucey, who did much more than bring me into this world and raise me up in it.

Over time, they also helped me recognize a void in my professional career, a need in the financial services industry to focus more attention on the importance of Social Security in a comprehensive retirement plan. They started me on a journey many years ago when Social Security was not a typical planning concern for clients and their financial advisors as they gathered around the conference table.

Nor would this book have been possible without my wife, Patty, who prefers I keep my heartfelt appreciation for her contributions to a minimum. Let me just state briefly how much I appreciate her support, especially in allowing me to skip out on too many household duties in order to build my own business and support our family for almost twenty-five years.

Special thanks to my son, Gavin, who allows me to vicariously indulge in my love of hockey through his own budding youth career. He continually reminds me why family is important.

To my professional colleagues and mentors whose advice and guidance have been invaluable in the building and expansion of my practice:

To Ed Slott, a not-so-secret weapon whose expertise has given me an advantage in the ever-changing world of finance, especially when it comes to dealing with some of the more complicated issues of tax planning and Social Security.

To Larry Kotlikoff and Mary Beth Franklin, resources I've relied on frequently over the years to provide answers to my questions involving the intricacies of Social Security.

To the group at Covisum, whose knowledge of Social Security and software products dealing with it provided the background for much of what I know of the subject today.

To the team and family of advisors I've met at Advisors Excel who continually help me grow my practice and support families with financial planning.

Special thanks also to the team at iHeartRadio, which for the past eight years has helped me voice my thoughts and philosophy throughout the Minneapolis-Saint Paul area via my Saturday morning radio program on Twin Cities NewsTalk AM 1130.

A salute as well to my brothers and sisters in the United States Marine Corps, which taught me the value of tough love in learning to be a leader and a builder. Semper Fi!

To my staff at Secured Retirement Financial, without whom I would not be able to help the families who depend on us. You know who you are, and you know how much I appreciate your good work.

To the writers, Kristen Gordon and Rick Dean, who spent hours helping me write and rewrite the words you read here and in various other media forums. Also to my editor, Bill Kentling, whose feedback and deadlines were instrumental in this book's completion.

Finally, to my valued clients—the people I am graced to help with their financial planning and Social Security concerns—my most sincere thanks. I only hope to continue helping them through the years of research I've done in trying to fill the void first noted by my parents.

About the Author

Joe Lucey is a Certified Financial Planner™ and Registered Financial Consultant who leads a team of advisors as president of Minneapolis-based Secured Retirement Financial. With nearly twenty-five years experience in the financial services arena, his Secured Retirement Blueprint™ process has helped several thousand families achieve a secure and independent retirement through comprehensive financial planning.

He is a frequent contributor in various media forums, among them hosting the weekly "Secured Retirement Radio" program that airs on TwinCities Newstalk AM1130 on Saturday mornings. He is a nationally recognized "RetireMentor" for Dow Jones-owned MarketWatch online. He is a frequent contributing author on retirement planning issues with insights and strategies geared to the objectives, concerns, risks, and opportunities facing retirees and those transitioning into retirement. He also is a member of the Ed Slott Master Elite IRA Advisor Group.

Outside of work, he enjoys spending time with his wife Patty and son Gavin, who shares his father's love of hockey. He and his family are active in their church and community through projects such as Make-A-Wish, Second Harvest, Fisher House, and the

Minnesota Military Family Foundation. He is an active supporter of youth hockey and a season-ticket holder of the NHL's Minnesota Wild.

Contact

While I wrote this book to help you begin thinking through your Social Security decisions and the numerous ways your choices will play into your greater retirement income picture, this is by no means an exhaustive look at your personal situation. If you have more questions and would like to work with a financial professional who can give you a more comprehensive overview of your finances, give me a call. Whether you are a fit to work with me or whether you might benefit from a referral, I'm here to help:

Joe Lucey
Secured Retirement Financial
www.securedretirements.com
Phone: (952) 460-3260 | Fax: (952) 460-3261
info@securedretirements.com

5775 Wayzata Blvd, Ste 830
St. Louis Park, MN 55416

60301510R00074

Made in the USA
Columbia, SC
15 June 2019